TAKE
DOMINION

TAKE DOMINION

BOB WEINER
with DAVID WIMBISH

Published by
chosen books

FLEMING H. REVELL COMPANY
OLD TAPPAN, NEW JERSEY

Scripture quotations identified NAS are from *The New American Standard Bible,* copyright © The Lockman Foundation 1960, 1962, 1963, 1968, 1971, 1972, 1973, 1975, 1977.

Scripture quotations identified NIV are from *The Holy Bible, New International Version,* copyright © by the International Bible Society, used by permission of Zondervan Bible Publishers.

Scripture quotations identified KJV are from the King James Version of the Bible.

LIBRARY OF CONGRESS
Library of Congress Cataloging-in-Publication Data

Weiner, Bob.
   Take dominion / Bob Weiner with David Wimbish.
   p. cm.
   ISBN 0-8007-9119-3
   1. Christian life—1960–   2. Evangelistic work. 3. Maranatha
Christian Churches. 4. Weiner, Bob. I. Wimbish, David.
II. Title.
BV4501.2.W4165 1988
269'.2—dc19   87-35450
                                            CIP

A Chosen Book
Copyright © 1988 by Bob Weiner

Chosen Books are published by
Fleming H. Revell Company
Old Tappan, New Jersey
Printed in the United States of America

This book is lovingly dedicated to
Earline Steelberg and her late husband, Wesley
Albie and Helen Pearson
Bob Sr. and Gerrie Weiner, my parents

Contents

Contents

Foreword

Before I met Bob Weiner, I met a number of young men and women he inspired with the Gospel of the Lord Jesus Christ. There was something different about these kids. They were consumed with being instruments for God.

Then, when I met Bob Weiner, I understood what it was about these kids that was so exciting. Bob was talking about being sold out to the Lord, one hundred percent committed to Jesus Christ.

I didn't know we could do that! But the more I listened to Bob, the more I understood what he was saying. And the more I knew he was one hundred percent right. In order to be effective for God, we need to die to ourselves.

I've read many of Bob's Bible study books and have been blessed by how the Lord has used him and his wife, Rose, to teach godly principles, how to study the Word of God, and how to be full of God. Bob has blessed many people and will bless many more. He is dynamite! He is filled with fire and his heart is set on winning the world to the Lord Jesus Christ.

It has been my privilege and pleasure to be in many meetings in which Bob has spoken, and each time I am compelled to do *more* because of the fire that is in him.

The Spirit of God that operates in Bob is catchy. I know that this book will bless you tremendously because God is using Bob to teach us how to be better sons and daughters of the Lord Jesus.

The young people of Maranatha have caught God's vision that He has given through Bob Weiner: that winning the world for Jesus Christ is not only possible but it will be accomplished. Bob stirs up the hearts of young people to make a difference in our world today. I praise God for the opportunity to work right alongside of him!

Rosey Grier
Los Angeles, California

TAKE
DOMINION

Chapter One

Incident on a Florida Highway

It was the sort of day nobody expects in Florida, even in the middle of February. It was cold, windy, and rainy. In short, it was miserable.

I had been in Orlando on business and was just beginning the two-hour drive back to my home in Gainesville. Traffic was crawling along, since most Floridians are not at all used to driving in those conditions.

Then I saw him.

A young man was standing by the side of the road, just ahead, with his thumb stuck out. I couldn't tell much about him, except that he was definitely not dressed for that kind of weather. He was wearing a thin windbreaker sort of jacket, and I knew he had to be soaked to the bone.

I looked around at the interior of my brand-new car. It was spotless, just the way I like to keep it.

"Well," I reasoned with myself, "I'm probably not really headed in the direction he's going. And besides, somebody's bound to feel sorry for him and pick him up before too long."

And then I felt a gentle nudge deep down in my spirit, the way I've felt it hundreds of times before. I knew immediately that God was telling me to stop and give this young man a ride.

Once again I looked around at the spotless interior of my car. "But Lord, do You really . . .?" Before the question was fully formed in my mind I knew the answer. God was indeed telling me to stop, and I knew I had to obey. In my mind, I saw the image of another young man hitchhiking, perhaps fifteen or twenty years ago.

"Yes, Lord," I said. "I remember what it was like to be out in the freezing rain, trying to catch a ride."

I was almost past him by now, but cut sharply out of the traffic, stopped perhaps fifteen yards in front of him, reached over and popped open the door on the passenger side. He continued to stand there for a moment, as if he couldn't believe I was really stopping for him. Then he picked up his backpack and came running.

When he got to the car, I could see he had been out in the cold rain a long time. His long, scraggly hair was wet and his clothes were drenched. He tossed his backpack into the backseat, then climbed into the front seat, getting muddy footprints all over the carpeting in the process. He looked to be in his mid-teens.

"Son," I said, "today is the day of salvation for you!"

I don't know what sort of reaction I expected, but my young passenger buried his face in his hands and began to cry deep, racking sobs.

"What's the matter, son?"

"You wouldn't believe it," he sobbed.

"Where are you headed?"

He shrugged his shoulders and continued to cry.

"Well then," I said as I reached over and turned the heater up a notch, "I'm heading to Gainesville, so you might as well come along."

He nodded in agreement, and we rode along in silence for a few minutes while I waited for him to compose himself.

Finally he spoke. "What was that you said when you picked me up?" he asked.

"I told you that today is the day of salvation for you."

"What did you mean?"

"I meant that God had spoken to me and told me to pick

you up." I pulled a handkerchief out of my pocket and handed it to him. "You do believe in God, don't you?"

"I do now," he answered. And then he poured out his story. His name was Rob, he said, and he had come to Florida from Ohio just a few days ago. Back home in Ohio he just hadn't been able to get along with his parents. They never seemed to understand him.

It had all come to a head this week when his parents had told him they couldn't put up with his lifestyle any longer. He claimed they wanted him out of their house and out of their lives.

Rob had thrown a few things into his backpack—the few items he considered the necessities of life—and had headed off in the direction of paradise, which to his young mind also went by the name of Florida. He had envisioned Florida as a land of bright sunshine and palm trees dancing in a warm, tropical breeze. Instead, he had found northern Florida to be a land of sometimes-freezing temperatures and harsh, driving winds.

"It took me three days to get here," he said, "and I haven't had a bite to eat in all that time."

He looked at his wristwatch. "I've forgotten exactly how long I've been standing out in the rain today, trying to catch a ride—six or seven hours, at least. But nobody would stop." His voice began to break with emotion, and he fought to regain his composure. I didn't say a word, but waited instead for him to finish his story.

"Finally," he went on, "I got so depressed I decided I was going to kill myself.

"Now I don't know God," he said, "and this next part is what I really can't believe. But I decided to pray and ask Him if He would help me. I said, 'God, if You're really there, please have the very next car stop for me. Because if You don't, I'm going to throw myself in front of the next car that comes along.' And I meant it, too! And then you . . . you . . ." He couldn't get the rest of it out.

"I was the next car that came along?"

He nodded.

"Well, Rob," I told him, "God really did tell me to stop for you. He loves you, you know."

"I really don't know anything about Him," Rob said.

"You know enough about Him to know that He told me to stop for you. You must know that He cares about you."

As we continued driving through the cold rain, I began telling my new acquaintance all about the God who loved him. I told him that God loved him enough to send His only Son to earth to die for him. I told him that the same God who had sent me to save him from taking his own life sent Jesus Christ to save him from his sins and give him eternal salvation. I explained that God had a plan for his life and didn't want him to throw it away.

By the time I finished explaining all this to Rob, he had decided he wanted to turn his life over to Jesus Christ.

"Are you sure?" I asked him. "This isn't something you can do now and then change your mind about later. If you surrender your life to Christ you have to mean it. You have to give control of your life to Him and live the way He wants you to live."

"I'm sure," he told me. "I'm only sixteen, and I've already made a mess out of my life trying to do things my way."

I led him in a simple prayer of repentance and faith in Jesus Christ, and an immediate and startling transformation took place before my eyes. A heavy burden seemed to lift from his shoulders. He sat up straighter in the seat. He was smiling where he had been crying a few minutes before. And it was as if a light had snapped on in his eyes.

We talked for more than two-and-a-half hours and by the time we arrived in Gainesville, Florida, Rob had decided he wanted to be baptized. After further discussion, I determined that he understood clearly what I had shared with him and that he understood the significance of the act of baptism.

Rob was baptized that very night. We also stopped along the road to get him something to eat, and Rob ate enough food to make up for his three days of doing without. Then I took him to a former fraternity house—now a Maranatha Campus Ministry chapel—near the University of Florida, where he would be able to stay for the next few days. The fraternity house was owned by Maranatha Campus Ministries. The house was used for church meetings, and the second floor was residence for some members of our campus fellowship.

Over the next few days Rob attended several Bible study sessions. He also called his parents to talk things over with them. He apologized for the things he had done to cause their anger, and they in turn told him that they were sorry. They were delighted to hear of the change in Rob's lifestyle and asked him to come home.

On the day he left Gainesville, Rob seemed to be a totally different young man from the one who had been hitchhiking in the rain a few days before.

Rob knew that things would be different at home this time, and so did I.

Rob's story is an amazing one—but it's also a familiar one to me. I've seen many similar life-changing incidents. And I am convinced that if you know how to listen to the promptings of the Holy Spirit and are willing to obey God without questioning Him, your life will become a series of exciting adventures, and you will see lives changed all around you . . . not because of what you do, but because of what God will do through you.

If your life isn't that way, it can be. It not only can be, it ought to be. And that's what this book is all about—turning your life into an exciting daily adventure with God. I want to share with you some of the things God has done in my life, and help you understand how He can do the same things in yours. God has told us to bring salvation to the lost and to change this world for the better.

This book is designed to help you get on with the most exciting adventure of your life!

Chapter Two

The Early Years

I had always believed in striving for excellence and in attempting to do your best for God—but this was ridiculous!

In fact, when Tony first suggested it, I thought he was kidding. My response was to throw back my head and laugh. But then I noticed Tony wasn't laughing with me. He was serious about this!

I was a sergeant in the Air Force at the time, stationed in the desert community of Victorville, California. But most of my nights and weekends were spent in San Bernardino where, among other things, I helped manage a Christian coffeehouse. It was 1969 and our coffeehouse featured, along with music, blacked-out windows and black-light rooms with Christian posters.

We would entertain the teenage crowd by giving them sodas and letting them listen to music, and then I would get up on stage—shaking like a leaf—and present the Four Spiritual Laws. I was no dynamic preacher and wasn't really even sure of my own total commitment to God. But still, every time we opened the doors, the kids would crowd the place, and we'd have a dozen or more deciding to commit their lives to Christ.

It was a Friday afternoon, early in the fall—one of the hottest days of Indian summer, and we were expecting a big crowd that night. We had several of the most popular local bands coming in and that meant up to four or five hundred kids could be spending the evening with us. It was going to be one of our biggest nights of the year.

I left the base early and arrived in San Bernardino about four P.M. When I walked into the coffeehouse it was absolutely stifling inside. It was 105 degrees outside and like a steam bath inside. I made my way through the building to the switch for the antiquated air-conditioning system.

But when I flipped the big switch I got a very unpleasant surprise: Nothing happened.

I flipped it off and on again. Nothing.

Perhaps a circuit breaker had been tripped.

But a quick check of the breakers showed me that everything was as it should be.

"Oh, Lord," I moaned, "what am I going to do?"

Well . . . there was only one thing to do. That was to look in the yellow pages under *Air-conditioning repairs*. I called the first company on the list, explained my predicament, and was assured that a repairman would be on the scene within a half-hour.

When the repairman arrived, we went around to the back of the building to the huge air-conditioning unit. It didn't take him long to make a diagnosis.

"I'm sorry," he said, "but there's nothing I can do. This thing is completely shot."

"You mean, you— "

"Take my word for it," he said. "At least two of these motors are completely burned out—and maybe a third."

He started to tell me how much it would cost to repair the system, but I stopped him. It didn't matter how much it was, because there was no way we could afford it. The coffeehouse was a labor of love; it certainly wasn't bringing in any money.

Besides, how could I be sure that the repairman wasn't just trying to take me for a ride? He'd probably make a pretty good commission on a repair job of that size.

So I thanked him for coming and watched him climb back into his truck and drive off.

As soon as he was gone, I called the second company listed in the yellow pages and asked how soon they could send a repairman out. By five-thirty he was on the scene. Unfortunately, his diagnosis was the same as the first repairman. In fact, he was even more severe.

"This thing," he told me flatly, "will never work again." He went so far as to suggest that what we really needed was a totally new unit!

I knew that was all there was to it. We'd have to close the coffeehouse—not only for tonight, but probably for good. After all, we were always using the air-conditioning, even sometimes in the middle of winter.

Tony arrived just as the second repairman was driving off. Tony was seventeen, a student at one of the local high schools and a young man who was really excited about God. He was a regular at the coffeehouse and often came by early, just as he was doing today, to help us get ready. I was standing in front of the building when he walked up.

"Hi, Bob!" he greeted me enthusiastically. "Ready for the big night tonight?"

"Oh, hi, Tony. Looks like I've got some bad news for you."

"What's wrong?"

"The air conditioner is shot. And it's as hot as an oven in there. . . . No, hotter."

"Can't you get it fixed?"

I shook my head. "I've had two repairmen out here already, and both of them tell me there's nothing they can do. In fact, we'll probably have to shut the place down."

"But you can't do that."

"What else can we do?" I shrugged and slapped him on the back. "Well, come on. You can help me call the bands and tell them not to show up."

"Hmmmmm. Listen, Bob . . . "

"Yeah?"

"The Bible says that we can lay hands on the sick and see them recover."

"Yeah, I know that."

"Well . . . I have faith that if we lay hands on this air-conditioning system, it will work."

That's when I laughed.

When I stopped laughing, I saw that he was totally serious.

"Come on, Tony, you don't really think— "

"Yes, I do." He gave me a look that seemed to question my faith in God. "It doesn't make any sense for this to happen. This place is going to be packed tonight. There's no telling how many kids will wind up giving their lives to the Lord. I'm convinced He'll fix the air-conditioning for us."

"Listen, Tony," I told him, "I really appreciate your faith, but I just don't think— "

"Won't you even try it?"

I rolled my eyes toward heaven and sighed. "Okay. You win. It won't hurt to try."

Once again I found myself in back of the building, facing the crippled air-conditioning system. I tried to summon up faith, but it was hard to do when I felt so silly.

"Okay, Bob," Tony urged me. "Put your hands up here on this thing."

I looked around to see if anyone was going to see me. This was embarrassing.

"Bob?"

"Okay, Tony. I'm doing it. See?"

He nodded and put his hands on the unit, too. Then he closed his eyes and said, "In the name of Jesus, I command this air-conditioning unit to work."

That was it.

"Now," he said. "Let's go turn this thing on and see what happens."

I didn't say anything, but I was thinking, *Poor kid. This is probably going to hurt his faith.*

I hesitated for just a second before I pulled the giant switch down to the *on* position. But when I did, I was the one who

22

got the shock of my life. The unit roared into action and began pumping cold air!

I just looked at Tony.

"Thank You, Jesus," he said. And then we were jumping around, shouting, and praising God.

When we were finished, Tony had a few more words for me: "See, Bob, if God can heal the sick, He can certainly repair a machine!"

That night the place was packed. The bands were excellent and I could sense the presence of God's Spirit throughout the evening. When at the end of the night I got up on stage to talk about the Lord, I had something new to talk about. The kids were blown away when I told them how our air-conditioning had been "healed" by the laying on of hands and prayer.

The Christians in the audience, of course, were excited by this demonstration of God's power. But the ones who were really touched were the non-Christians—the kids who had just come to listen to the music and be part of the action.

I don't remember exactly how many responded to our altar call that night, but it was many more than usual. And I had tears in my eyes when I thought about how close I had come to canceling the program.

This Tony was some kind of Christian. And the God we served was some kind of God. I made up my mind that night that I wanted to be more like Tony. I also made up my mind that I would never again doubt God's Word.

And I can tell you one thing I have seen demonstrated many times over since then: God's Word is absolutely true! You can bet your life on it.

I've always known about God. As far back as I can remember, growing up in the Chicago area, I attended church with my parents. I was always there for Sunday school, Vacation Bible School, you name it. I will always be thankful for that spiritual foundation. But at the same time, I'll have to admit that the God I knew back in those days wasn't a very exciting one. I knew that He cared about me and that He would always be there for me. But He was far off in the distance, a benign Father figure who didn't really present much of a challenge as far as my day-to-day life went.

My fuzzy conception of God is the main reason, I suppose, that my commitment to Him was never what it ought to have been. Even in my early twenties, when I was witnessing to others about the Lord and managing the Christian coffee-house, I was still struggling to live the Christian life. And I knew that my own commitment to Christ was lukewarm, at best. I wanted to be a Christian, but the Christian life was rather boring. Today I understand that there is nothing the least bit boring about it—that it's one challenge after another, one exciting adventure after another. If you haven't yet discovered that, I believe you will by the time you get to the end of this book. But more about that later.

I know now, too, that even before I was born, God was preparing me to be a minister of His Gospel. When I was just a baby, for instance, my Jewish father and my mother were saved. From that time on, my parents were actively involved in serving the Lord and we never missed a service at the Evangelical Free church we attended. My mother's grand-father, who was also Jewish, was saved under Billy Sunday's ministry in Chicago and later went with the Billy Sunday team setting up tents and helping in whatever way he could. Also my mother's great-grandfather was a circuit rider.

So it would seem that heritage plays an important part in God's plans for our lives. In my Jewish family, for instance, there has been a close contact with Christianity over the years, and the Lord has honored that.

And I am sure my heritage is a large part of the reason that January 1965—four years before our coffeehouse days—found me enrolling in Trinity College, an evangelical Christian school in Chicago. I thought I was a good Christian at the time, but in retrospect I really wasn't. I wanted to know God but didn't see anybody really fired up the way I thought a real Christian should be. I got frustrated and started rebelling. I probably wasn't the worst student Trinity ever had, insofar as being a troublemaker. But on the other hand, I know I turned more than a few hairs on professors' heads gray. I have never been the type to take no for an answer; nor, until I really came to know the Lord, was I likely to take somebody's word for something that I hadn't proven for myself. My aggressive personality landed me in some unusual predicaments and, for a while at least, turned me into something of a legend at Trinity College.

That happened while I was in Washington, D.C., with the Trinity College Touring Choir.

We were touring the city, visiting the congressional offices, and singing in some of the area churches. I had picked up a gold pass from the Vice-President's office and was sitting in the V.P.'s area in the Senate gallery, watching the proceedings on the floor below. Much to my surprise, one of the young pages came up to me with a message. The note read: "Someone in the Senate recognizes you and will be up to talk to you as soon as he has a chance."

My reaction, naturally, was, "Who in the world knows me in the United States Senate?"

Before too long, I saw the head page heading my way.

"Bob Weiner! How you doing, old buddy?"

"Cliff? Cliff Stone?"

Cliff was an old friend of mine from Oak Lawn, Illinois. I hadn't seen him in years and had no idea he was in Washington. I could tell from the way the other pages deferred to him that Cliff was doing all right. And he wanted to show me that he had some clout around Washington.

After we talked for a while, he said, "Bob, anywhere you want to go in Washington, anything you want to see, you just let me know and I'll arrange it for you." Then he took me all around the Capitol, showing me several rooms that were normally off-limits to tourists.

Then he said, "Listen, Bob, how'd you like to go on a tour of the State Department? Nobody ever gets to go over there!"

I wasn't really that excited about looking around at the main State Department building, but the fact that "nobody ever gets to go over there" made it more appealing. So Cliff summoned a limousine, and a friend from the choir and I found ourselves headed to the State Department.

When we got there, I walked in and spoke to the man at the security desk.

"Hi! I'm Bob Weiner and I'm here to take a tour."

"Oh, I'm sorry, Mr. Weiner," he said, "but the President and the Vice-President are up on on the top floor having dinner with some foreign dignitaries. We're not allowing anyone into the building. Mr. Stone didn't know about the dinner or he wouldn't have sent you here. He's asked me to please extend his apologies."

Hmmmm. Dinner with the President. That sounded interesting.

"Okay, thank you," I said. "I was wondering . . . is there another exit?"

"Sure," he said, pointing across the lobby. "You can go right out that door."

"Okay. Thank you very much."

My friend and I walked across the long lobby to the other exit, and I noticed just before we got to the door a set of elevators. I looked around and saw that the security guard was turned the other way. With my friend in tow, I ran over and punched the elevator button. The doors opened immediately, I dragged my friend in and pushed the button for the top floor.

"Are you crazy?" he demanded. "What do you think you're doing?"

"Don't you want to have dinner with the President?"

"No. And I don't want to spend the rest of my life eating prison food, either!"

"Come on, where's your spirit of adventure?"

The elevator let us out on the seventh floor and my friend didn't know what else to do, so he followed me.

"Hey, look!" I told him. "It's the Secretary of State's office."

We walked up to the receptionist. My friend looked as though he was trying to hide behind me.

"Hi," I said, "how you doing?"

"Fine, thank you."

"I'm Bob Weiner," I began, acting as if it were the most

natural thing in the world for me to be there. "I'm with the Trinity College Choir, and we're taking a tour of Washington. And I was wondering if Dean Rusk is in. We'd like to say hello."

She smiled. "I'm sorry," she said, "but he isn't in. He's attending a dinner with the President up on the top floor." Hmmm. So that elevator could go higher if you knew how to work it.

"Well, do you think we could go in and see his office? Maybe sit in his chair for a minute, just so we could say we've been there?"

To my surprise, she shrugged and said, "Why not?"

My friend was too nervous to take a turn sitting in Rusk's chair. All he wanted to do was to get out of there. But I was having a great time.

"Just think," I said to the receptionist, "I'm sitting in the Secretary of State's chair! Tell me, is there any way we could get up to that dinner, just to see what's going on?"

"No, I'm afraid not. You have to have a special security key to get up there, and the dinner is by invitation only."

"Well, thank you very much," my friend said. "We have to be going now. Let's go, Bob."

"Yes . . . well, like he said, we'd better be running along. Thanks again."

"You're welcome. You enjoy the rest of your time here."

Out in the hall I spotted something intriguing: a freight elevator.

"Hey! Do you suppose that thing goes up to the top floor?"

"I don't know and I don't care." He had had enough of my impulsive actions.

"Well, I just thought that— "

"You do what you want," he snapped, as he pushed the button for the elevator we had come in. "I'm getting out of here." He hit the button again in an attempt to speed up the elevator's arrival.

As for me, I had come this far and I wasn't going to give up now.

As it turned out, my hunch was correct: the freight elevator did go all the way to the top. I got in, pushed the button, and began my ascent to the elite eighth floor.

When the door opened, I saw a dozen or more people hurrying back and forth in front of me dressed in chefs' hats, wearing aprons, and so on. I was in the kitchen! I also saw an armed policeman standing guard right in front of the elevator. What could I do now? Then it hit me. I still had that gold pass from the Vice-President's office, and I was wearing my best blue suit. Maybe if I flashed the gold card as I walked past the policeman, he'd think I was one of the dinner guests.

That's exactly what I did, and it worked. He didn't say a word to me. But there was another obstacle. As I came out of the kitchen, I saw another guard—a soldier in full-dress uniform, standing in front of a huge pair of doors leading into the ballroom. I figured the best thing to do in a situation like this was to be bold, so I walked right up to him.

"Excuse me, sir," I said. "I know I'm a little late to the party, but could you show me where I might find a seat?"

He opened the door for me and pointed. "Sure. There are some seats right over there."

I strode in and sat down. I was at the far end of the hall, but up at the head table sat President Lyndon Johnson, Vice-President Hubert Humphrey, Secretary of State Rusk, and several dignitaries from Upper Volta, Africa—including that republic's president.

I got in on the very tail end of the festivities, but I heard enough to know who the Africans were, and that they spoke French. As soon as the dinner had been dismissed, I headed for the front table to see if I could meet Lyndon Johnson or Hubert Humphrey. But by the time I walked all the way around to the front table, the President and the Vice-President were deep in conversation with the president of Upper Volta and some other official-looking people. But two other men, whom I later found out were the heads of the military and the National Assembly of Upper Volta, were standing by themselves. I had studied two years of French, so I thought I'd go over and try to talk to them.

"Bonjour, Messeigneurs," I said. Then, in what was

undoubtedly not the most fluent French they had ever heard, I told them I was Bob Weiner and that I was here to greet them as a representative from the youth of America. "We are so happy to have you here as our friends," I finished.

This excited them, and they began calling for their president to join us. "Presidente! Presidente! We want you to meet Robert! He is here to tell you how happy the young people of America are that you are visiting their country!" They were positively beaming as their leader, escorted by Dean Rusk, came over to join us.

By this time I could see that my French was not going to be sufficient to hold a conversation, so I resorted to an interpreter. The president began to ask me all sorts of questions about the youth of America, especially concerning "our" views on international affairs—and I suddenly realized I had become the center of attention. President Johnson and Vice-President Humphrey were standing off to the side, but everyone was gathering around listening to the conversation between the president of Upper Volta and me!

Before long a waiter came and gave us all demitasse cups. A few minutes later another came by and handed everyone a cigar. Suddenly I was beginning to feel extremely nervous. What on earth was Dean Rusk thinking?

Finally I told my newfound African friends that it was time to part. I shook hands with them all and turned around and walked away. How was I going to get out of here? I didn't even know where the real elevator was!

I went through a door I thought might lead to the elevator. Instead I found myself standing out on a balcony with Lady Bird Johnson, who was getting a bit of fresh air.

She turned and smiled at me. "Hello. How are you doing today?"

For a minute I couldn't think of what to call her. Was it Mrs. President? Your majesty? Lady Bird? Or perhaps just Lady? Maybe plain old Mrs. Johnson was my best bet.

"Oh, I'm fine, thank you, Mrs. Johnson. By the way, do you know where the elevator is?"

"Sure, it's right over there," and she pointed me in the right direction.

Whew! I jumped in just as the doors were closing.

And then I froze. There were several people already in it—the Secretary of State and all the dignitaries from Upper Volta—plus several tough-looking guys who had to be Secret Service agents.

There was nothing else to do at this point, so I just stood calmly without saying a word. As soon as we got to the ground floor, I'd just go in whichever direction they weren't going and things would be fine.

But another surprise awaited me when we got to the bottom.

Word had spread around that the President and other dignitaries would be coming out of this elevator, and there was a large crowd waiting for us, including most of the members of the Trinity College Choir. At least a dozen mouths dropped open simultaneously when they saw me come out of the elevator surrounded by all these statesmen! What made it even more difficult for me was that there was no way of escape.

A roll of red velvet carpet had been spread across the floor for us to walk on. Theater poles had been set up all along both sides of the carpet, with velvet ropes to hold back the crowds. I had no choice but to follow the carpeting. Maybe once we got outside I could make a break for it.

No such luck. The carpeting led straight to a shiny black limousine, and since I was the first one in line, the driver opened the door for me and motioned for me to enter the car.

So I did.

But as soon as I did, I scooted all the way across the back seat, opened the other door, got out as fast as I could, and disappeared into the crowd along the street.

When the choir finally got back to Trinity College, my "hobnobbing" with the leaders of our country had become the hot topic of conversation, and I had become a red-faced celebrity!

Amazingly enough, an almost identical thing happened to

me just a little over a year later. Although, given my aggressive personality and inclination to barge into places I didn't belong, I suppose it wasn't amazing at all.

This time I was walking down a street in Chicago when I was confronted by a group of antiwar protesters marching along toward me. I walked up to one of the women in the group and asked her where they were going. She told me they were headed for McCormick Place because the President was supposed to be there attending a dinner.

"Why don't you come along?" she added.

"Well, I don't really believe in what you're doing," I told her. "But sure, I'll walk along with you. I'd like to see what happens."

What happened, once we got close to McCormick Place, was that the police moved in and started harassing the marchers, trying to keep them as far away from the building as possible. It was an easy matter for me, since I was wearing a suit and didn't fit in with the rest of this scraggly, hippie-looking crowd, to slip away and walk right around the policemen.

I walked over to the front of McCormick Place, where elegantly dressed couples were beginning to arrive, and found out that a thousand-dollar-a-plate dinner was about to begin. Not only would the President be in attendance, but so would Chicago Mayor Richard Daley, Illinois Senator Everett Dirksen, and a host of other VIPs and celebrities. Hmmmm. . . . Wouldn't it be something if I could get inside?

After watching a while longer, I realized that as the couples arrived, they showed a pass to the doorman, who then let them inside. The doorman was not scrutinizing the passes all that closely.

I waited for the next couple, and as soon as they headed for the door, I walked right up to them and acted as though I'd known them for years.

"Why, hello!" I gushed. "You remember me. Bob Weiner?" As I was talking I fell into step beside them. The man flashed his invitation at the doorman, and the three of us walked on inside the lobby.

Once we were safely inside, the woman said, "Bob Weiner? Should I know you?"

"Oh, well . . . I'm not sure. Maybe I'm mistaken. Please excuse me."

But by that time we were on our way up the escalator to the main reception area.

When I got there, I was facing obstacle number two. You needed a second ticket to get into the reception area, and once again I didn't have one. Lines were forming at several desks where people were picking up their tickets. I wasn't sure what to do, but figured I'd get in line anyway. Perhaps by the time I got to the front of the line I'd have a plan.

The couple just in front of me gave me the answer.

"Our senator will have our tickets when he gets here," they said, "so can we just sign for them now?"

"Surely. Go right ahead."

"Uh . . . hello, ma'am," I said to the woman at the desk. "I'm Bob Weiner. I guess Senator Dirksen isn't here yet. Can I go ahead and sign for my ticket now?"

"Sure you can, Mr. Weiner." She had me sign my name on her list; then she handed me a pass, good for admittance into the main reception area.

"Thank you."

I was no more than five or six steps away from her desk when she called after me, "Oh, Mr. Weiner, here's Senator Dirksen now!" I pretended not to hear her and hurried on into the reception area, where I quickly lost myself in the crowd.

The room was full of national and local celebrities. The elegant suits and sparkling dresses let me know I was in the middle of a very elite gathering. The first thing I wanted to do was look for a pay phone so I could call my parents.

"Hi, Dad," I said, when he answered the phone. "You'll never guess where I am!" I couldn't tell whether he was appropriately impressed, but he seemed nervous about the way I had obtained entrance into the reception.

"What are you going to do now?" he asked.

"I'm going to see if I can find someone who'll give me a

ticket to the thousand-dollar-a-plate dinner so I can eat!" I replied.

Dad laughed at that, and I don't blame him. It didn't seem likely that some stranger would just hand me a ticket.

I picked out several likely-looking couples and asked, "Say, you wouldn't happen to have an extra ticket for the dinner, would you?" The response was always the same: "Are you kidding? It took us months to save up enough to buy our tickets!"

On the other hand, I had always figured that the old saying is true, "Where there's a will, there's a way." I had the will; all I needed to do was find the way.

Finally I saw a large group of people gathered around one man, who was obviously someone important.

"Excuse me," I asked someone on the fringes. "Can you tell me who that man is?"

"Why, that's Judge Ferguson."

I'd heard the name. He was an influential judge within the city of Chicago. Perhaps he was my key! If I walked up to him in front of all these people and called him by name, maybe he'd pretend to recognize me.

And that's just what I did.

"Hey, Judge Ferguson! Remember me—Bob Weiner!"

"Bob Weiner?"

"Yes, sir. You know my dad—Bob Weiner, Sr. From the South Side."

"Oh, of course! Bob Weiner! How are you?"

I'm sure the judge assumed that my father was a big supporter, and it could be embarrassing, not to mention damaging politically, not to recognize the son of one of your biggest supporters.

But I didn't expect the extent of the judge's interest in me. He put his arm around me and announced, "Hey, everybody, this is Bob Weiner. His dad's a very good friend of mine!"

Then he turned to me. "How is your dad, anyway? Is he here?"

"No, no, he couldn't make it tonight."

As soon as I had a chance I said, "Listen, Judge Ferguson,

I've got a bit of a problem, and I was wondering if you might be able to help me out."

"Problem? What is it?"

"Well, you see, I wasn't able to get a ticket for the dinner tonight and I— "

"No problem," he said. And it wasn't. He not only got me a ticket, but insisted that I sit at his table!

The only problem was that his table was about two-thirds of the way back in the auditorium. So as soon as dinner was over, I excused myself and told him I was going to look for a better seat. Sure enough, there was an empty spot right in the front row, where I sat and listened to speeches by President Johnson, Mayor Daley, and other dignitaries.

Now, admittedly, my behavior in these two situations wasn't very Christlike. My Christianity at the time was not what it should have been. At the same time, I was exhibiting an attitude that under the Lordship of Jesus Christ has served me well in my Christian walk. Namely, I have resolved never to let circumstances rule my life. Rather, I try to find a solution in whatever circumstance or situation I find myself.

This was true in 1966 when I enlisted in the Air Force and found myself stationed in San Antonio, Texas.

I was amazed by the fact that the only thing all the other guys talked about was how much they wanted to go home as soon as basic training was over. Many of these guys had not seen anything of the world except their own hometowns, yet they seemed uninterested in seeing or learning anything new.

As for me, I thought the weeks between basic training and my first assignment would be a perfect occasion for visiting Mexico.

But when I told my sergeant what I wanted to do, he said I couldn't leave the country because I was a member of the United States Air Force. He didn't know why not, exactly; that's just the way it was.

There was a lieutenant I could talk to about it, he admitted when I asked, but it probably wouldn't do me any good.

I got the same story from the lieutenant, but he finally

agreed that I could talk to a colonel, who in turn sent me to the general in charge of the entire base.

"Sir, I'd love to see Mexico," I told him. "Can you give me special permission so I can leave the country?"

"Why do you want to go to Mexico?" he asked, looking surprised that anyone would make such a request.

"Well, sir, I've never been outside of the U.S. I came here straight from college, I've got four weeks, and I'd just like to see someplace I haven't been before. I'd love to see Mexico City."

He thought for a few moments. "We've never had a request like this before. But if you really want to see Mexico, I don't see why not." And he signed a paper giving me special permission to leave the United States.

I got on the bus at the Mexican border, wearing my Air Force uniform and carrying only a small bag of personal items. I didn't know a word of Spanish. But on the twenty-four-hour ride to the Mexican capital I made several Mexican friends, including a young woman about my age who had been in the United States visiting relatives.

We made good use of the bus trip: She taught me as much Spanish as I could absorb, and I helped her improve her English. By the time we reached Mexico City, she had invited me to spend my time there with her family.

I wound up having a wonderful visit. I enjoyed getting to know the people and their customs. My new friend's family showed me all around Mexico City. And her father, who turned out to be a fantastic tailor, even made me some beautiful clothes. There was a business suit, which I wore for several years, along with some shirts and a couple of pairs of pants—simply because of the hospitality and generosity of this man's heart.

Since that visit I have always had a deep love for people of different cultures. It has been one of my desires to get to know them, to eat at their tables, to share in their customs. The different cultures on this planet, I believe, are a marvelous demonstration of God's love and creative power.

So here I was, twenty years old, having finished two years

of college, enlisted in the Air Force, and traveled to Mexico City. Now I was sent off to George Air Force Base in Victorville, California. One of the first things I did there was to look for an apartment in San Bernardino. I knew I didn't want to have any more to do with the base than I had to. I felt it was very important not just to lie around the barracks for four years, murmuring and complaining about how tough Air Force life was, but to be productive and busy. I figured if life wasn't so great, do what you could to change it.

In San Bernardino, I had the good fortune to meet some men who would be instrumental in transforming my life.

The first of these was Bob Cording, a tremendously talented young man who was then working for Campus Crusade for Christ. I was fortunate to have Bob as a roommate. Bob in turn introduced me to Wes Hurd, who was also working for Campus Crusade. The two of them were running a coffeehouse in San Bernardino, and they asked me if I would like to help them.

Sure, I thought. *Why not?* I considered myself a Christian. I believed in Jesus and that He was the only way to God—and I wanted to do what I could to spread the message.

But there was something different about Cording and Hurd. They not only believed in Jesus, they were excited about Him. Whereas my attitude was, "Jesus will take care of me," their attitude was, "We want to change the world for Christ." For them, Christianity was an exciting, day-after-day adventure. They looked for the toughest challenges head-on and didn't seem to shrink from any of them.

The Bible says that whoever the Son makes free is free indeed, and Bob Cording was totally free! His lifestyle really amazed me. During this time he was editor of *Collegiate Challenge* magazine, and he put out some of the toughest, most creative issues of any magazine I've ever seen. He challenged existentialism and knew all the right ways to relate to young people.

When I started rooming with Bob, I wanted to be more like him. But I wasn't sure how to obtain his godliness for my own life. For instance, I was still smoking cigarettes in those days.

36

I wanted to quit, but just couldn't bring myself to do it. So, I never smoked at home. Instead, I'd go out for a walk so I could sneak a smoke. Then I'd take a quick shot of Listerine, hoping Bob wouldn't be able to tell what I'd been doing.

Another young man who really challenged my faith was Tony, the teenager who later prayed for God to heal our air-conditioning unit. That wasn't the only time I saw Tony in action. On another occasion, our coffeehouse, called The Other Door, was invaded by a group of Hell's Angels. We'd had such success among the young people of San Bernardino-Riverside that much of the drug traffic was drying up, and the Angels had let it be known they weren't happy about this.

We were just opening one evening when six of them—big, evil-looking guys—strode through the door, looking for all the world like gunslingers getting ready to tear down the saloon in a grade-B western. The management team gathered on the sidewalk outside to try to figure out what to do. Should we call the police? Attempt to throw them out? Try to reason with them?

While we were discussing all the available options, Tony walked up. Once again he was like some sort of guardian angel, arriving at just the right moment.

"We need to pray," he said.

"You're right, Tony. We do need to pray."

So we all held hands and stood in a circle, and Tony prayed. I was standing next to him, and as soon as he started praying, some sort of energy flowed out of him and into me. I don't know how to describe it except to say it was like electricity.

For a moment I forgot all about the Hell's Angels. All I could think was, *Man! This kid is really close to God!*

I was impressed, too, by the fact that he prayed with such authority. "In Jesus' name," he said, "we bind these Hell's Angels from destroying this coffeehouse, which is dedicated to reaching these young people for Christ. And we command them to come out of there now without causing any destruction."

It wasn't fifteen or twenty seconds later that all the Hell's Angels came walking out of the coffeehouse, climbed on their motorcycles, and rode off. They hadn't done any damage to the place and they never bothered us again. Even more amazing was the fact that as they filed out, they all reached into their pockets and dropped some money into the basket we had out to collect donations.

They had obviously come with destruction on their minds and wound up instead giving money toward our work—and none of us had said a single word to them. Chalk up another miraculous answer to prayer for Tony!

Then there was Albie Pearson, an ex-major league baseball player. He has always been a favorite of mine because he was a gritty, gutsy player who always gave his best effort. I admired him most of all, though, because of the fact that he was only 5'6" and he never let his height hold him back. He was proof that you didn't have to be six feet tall to be a big man in the world of sports—or in any other endeavor, for that matter.

When I was growing up in Chicago, Albie was a starter for the Washington Senators. Whenever the Senators were in town my dad tried to take me to one of the ball games. Albie had finished up his career with the California Angels and had stayed in southern California. What I didn't know as a boy was that Albie Pearson was also a dedicated Christian.

But when I read in the newspaper that he was going to be speaking in a youth rally at a Los Angeles area high school, I made plans to attend.

Apparently I wasn't the only Albie Pearson fan in the area, because the high school auditorium was packed. He gave an exciting, dynamic talk—all about what Jesus had done in his life, and how He could do the same thing in anyone else's life, too. I hung onto every word Pearson said. I was so close to what Albie, Bob, Wes, and Tony had—yet in some ways so far away.

In any case, I wanted to meet Albie Pearson, at least shake the hand of my old hero and tell him how much I appreciated his talk. So I waited in line for quite a while. I figured that by the time I got up to him he'd give me a quick handshake and that would be all. Instead, when he took my hand, Pearson looked me right in the eye.

"Young man," he said, "God has a great work he wants you to do. But you need more of Him in your life. And you need to be filled with God's Holy Spirit." Then he asked me if I would come over the following day, because he wanted to talk with me. He proceeded to give me directions to his house, which was more than thirty miles from San Bernardino.

I was excited because I knew the Lord was about to give me the big breakthrough I needed. I felt something was going to happen at Albie Pearson's house that would revolutionize my walk with God, and give me the same sort of power I saw in guys like Tony and Bob Cording. I was doubly excited to know that God was going to use a man like Albie Pearson, who had always been one of my heroes.

The next day, when I drove up to Albie's desert home, he and his wife seemed genuinely happy to see me. This couple was so in love with God that it almost seemed as if a light were shining in their eyes.

Albie told me that the minute he had seen me the evening before, God had impressed him that He wanted to use me in a special way and that I would be successful in reaching the youth of the nation. "But, Bob, you need more of God in your life. You need the power of His Holy Spirit!"

I agreed. I knew I needed something, and if he said it was the power of the Holy Spirit, then that was what I wanted.

We talked for a while. He opened his Bible and shared his thoughts with me for more than an hour. Then he asked if he could lay hands on me and pray for me.

"Please do!" I responded.

When he prayed that God would give me a special anointing of His Holy Spirit, I had the incredible feeling that my entire body was being revitalized, that every cell was being filled with a new source of energy. I felt calm, yet excited. I wanted to laugh and I wanted to cry. At that moment God seemed so real and close, I felt I could almost reach out and touch His face.

Before Albie prayed for me, I had always felt a duty to

witness to others about Christ. Afterward, I couldn't have stopped talking about the Lord if I had wanted to. And my witness took on a new effectiveness.

My first indication of this occurred back on the Air Force base. As newly elected secretary/treasurer of the Non-Commissioned Officers Association (I was now a sergeant), I was assigned to the wing commander's office when a group of new recruits came in to paint the office.

Almost immediately these men started talking about the meaning of life, wondering out loud what it was all about. Suddenly, for no reason whatever, they turned to me and began asking what I thought life was all about. Did I think life continued after death? And so on.

I couldn't believe it at first. Then I realized God was giving me a perfect opportunity to talk to them about His Son. Before I was through, four of these guys had asked me if they could accept Jesus as their Lord and Savior right there in the commander's office.

I didn't see why not, so we all got down on our knees and I led them in the sinner's prayer. During the middle of the prayer, the commander came in. But when he saw what was going on, he just smiled, went quietly back out the door, and waited outside until we were through.

The very next day, at the library in downtown San Bernardino, I entered into a conversation with a young man who was obviously desperately in need of a personal relationship with Jesus Christ.

When it became apparent that our conversation could not be conducted within the "quiet, please" confines of the library, we went outside. Within minutes, a group of teenagers had gathered around us, all of them wanting to know more about this Jesus.

I stood there on the library steps and preached to them, challenging them to commit their lives to Christ—and several of them, perhaps as many as a dozen, did just that.

It was more and more obvious that God was doing something wonderful in my life. Anywhere I went, people began asking me about Jesus!

Soon afterward, early in 1970, Bob Cording and I organized Sound Mind Productions, a company that promoted Christian concerts and other exciting enterprises. I would be getting out of the Air Force soon, and we wanted to intensify our efforts to reach the youth of Southern California. In addition to our work with the coffeehouses, we decided to put on concerts at the California Theater in San Bernardino with groups like Andrae Crouch and the Disciples, Love Song, and The Salt Company from Hollywood Presbyterian Church.

Andrae Crouch would bring his group to the concerts in three Volkswagen beetles; we could pay them only around three hundred dollars. They weren't getting rich coming all the way to San Bernardino to play for us, but none of them seemed to care. They were interested in seeing young people won to Christ, and if that happened they were happy.

In fact, one time we asked Andrae to do a concert when we didn't have any money to pay him at all. Bob Cording, who is a talented artist, promised he would design an album cover for Andrae in exchange for a concert. Andrae agreed to the deal, and Bob wound up designing the cover for the album *Live at Carnegie Hall.*

At times Satan tried to discourage us and close us down, but God would bring something good out of it. Like the time we scheduled a large outdoor concert at a city park with a group called The Brethren. The group featured Sherman Andrus, later of Andrus, Blackwood and Company. At the last minute, several of the residents near the park complained to the city council. They were afraid we were putting on a wild rock 'n' roll show and they didn't want it in their neighborhood, so the city revoked our permit for an outdoor concert.

We had to put signs up around the park saying, "The concert has been moved to the Civic Center," and the Civic Center was several miles away. We also had people driving around the park in trucks with signs on the sides, advising people of the change in the concert's location.

Not only did we get a huge crowd at the auditorium that night, but dozens of kids gave their lives to Jesus. The *San Bernardino Sun-Telegram* also sent a reporter and a photographer to cover the event. The paper wound up devoting a full page to the concert, including brief interviews with several of the concert-goers who were able to explain—in a secular newspaper—what Jesus Christ meant in their lives.

Despite Satan's attempt to spoil the concert, it turned out to be a time of real spiritual victory.

It was also a time when the Lord brought someone very special into my life.

Every summer, Campus Crusade for Christ held a student leadership conference at their headquarters in Arrowhead Springs, just north of San Bernardino. It's a beautiful mountainside setting, a place where you can really appreciate the beauty of God's creation.

On this particular occasion I was in a counseling room talking with a young couple about a problem they were having in their relationship when I looked up and saw her. She was a beautiful blonde, but it wasn't her appearance that struck me as much as the way I just knew immediately she was the one for me. She also seemed to be full of God; His glory was radiating out from her. Whoever she was, she had just finished praying with someone and was getting ready to leave.

My first inclination was to get up and run after her. I couldn't do that, of course, because I was still counseling the young couple. So I tried to get my mind back to the matter at hand. But even as I shared the Scriptures and prayed with them, I couldn't get this beautiful young woman out of my mind.

I was particularly convinced she was someone extra-special because I had quit going out with girls more than a year before. I had grown tired of the whole process of dating and had told the Lord I wanted to dedicate even that part of my life to Him. In fact, I had declared, "God, I don't even want to look at another girl until she's the one You have for me."

What I couldn't know now was that as soon as she walked out of the room she ran and found her roommate. Together they prayed that I would come and talk to them when I was finished with my counseling session.

And that's exactly what happened. I walked out of the room and went straight into the lobby where they were waiting for me. I introduced myself and discovered that her name was Rose Russell. Her father was a Methodist minister in Paducah, Kentucky, but Rose had resisted giving her life to Christ. In college she had tried to find herself in the fast whirl of sorority life and parties—until she encountered Campus Crusade for Christ. Then she learned that only God could bring meaning to life, and now she was totally committed to living for Him.

In fact, Rose had become known as something of a campus radical! Whenever the left-wing element appeared on campus trying to stir up revolution, she would go up and ask for a turn at the microphone. Then, instead of spouting the Marxist propaganda they expected, she'd start giving the positive proofs for the resurrection! She had become a powerful witness for Christ and had seen dozens of students won to the Lord in this way.

Rose and I had a great time getting to know each other over the next few weeks. As her time there ended and she went back to Kentucky to resume her job as a high school art teacher, I knew it would not be the end of our relationship.

As for me, my stint in the Air Force was over, so I moved to Long Beach, where I took a job with the Long Beach Visitors Guide and Map. My job was to go around to businessmen and get them to buy advertisements in the Guide, which was distributed free to visitors to the Long Beach area.

I didn't figure to be at this job too long, because Bob Cording and I still had a burning desire to reach the youth of our country. We knew the love of Jesus would make a tremendous difference on American campuses, and we were looking for the best way to take it there. This was the middle of 1970, and we were distressed by what was happening on our nation's college campuses. Antiwar protests were growing increasingly violent. Several administration buildings at a number of major universities were closed by student sit-ins. Some schools had been closed by student strikes. Then came the terrible tragedy at Kent State that left four students dead.

If any generation was ever desperate in its need to know Jesus Christ, surely it was this one.

Then one day, Bob Cording came to me with an idea. He had bought for $1,000 a 1919 Nash Touring Car that, it was believed, had once belonged to someone in Abraham Lincoln's family. The car was a surefire attention-getter. What we ought to do, he said, was pick up the car being stored near Chicago, then drive back across the country to California. On the way, we could stop at every major university campus and tell the young people that the only hope for our troubled society was the love of Jesus Christ.

I agreed with Bob. It sounded like a good idea to me, and we made plans to begin our trip early that fall. Bob also had the idea of printing thousands of copies of a newspaper called *Sound Mind*, to be distributed on the college campuses. Underground papers were popular all over the country, so it would be relatively easy to get the students to pick up ours. All we had to do was package the Gospel in a way that would relate to these students.

Bob had also met someone he wanted to go with us. Tom Rozof had been a hippie, strung out on drugs and "free love," when the Lord had saved him dramatically. He was now full of the love of God, and Bob was especially struck by the way he could relate to young people. He had long hair and a beard. In fact, he looked about the way one would expect Jesus to look!

Tom lived in a small Christian community called Big Bear, a rural area not too far from San Bernardino, and Bob invited me to come spend an evening there so I could get to know Tom better.

I was overwhelmed by what I found. I had never been around people so totally committed to God, who had given everything they had to him. Here all these people were living as one happy family, truly putting the other person before themselves, seeming not to seek their own satisfaction or gratification.

Bob and I were invited to stay for dinner with the people from the community; afterward we all joined together for a

Communion service. Then someone announced that it was time for the footwashing service.

"We always do this after dinner," Tom explained.

I didn't want to participate, because I was too proud, but Tom said I should wash Bob Cording's feet. As much as I thought of Bob, it was one of the hardest, most humbling things I have ever had to do. When Bob in turn began to wash my feet, I began to cry. Something inside of me—some vestiges of selfishness and pride—melted away, and I felt truly at peace with the Lord.

On our way home that evening, I told Bob I agreed with his choice. Tom was the perfect third man for our cross-country trip in the 1919 Nash that fall. It was going to be a wonderful adventure!

Back in Long Beach, it was hard to concentrate on my job as an ad salesman while waiting three months for our trip to begin.

One day, when I was feeling low and in need of some Christian fellowship, I looked up the number of the Rev. Wesley Steelberg, pastor of Christian Life Church in Long Beach. I could try to sell him an ad, but even if he didn't want to buy one, it would be a good chance to talk to a great man of God. I had heard many good things about Wesley Steelberg, and I knew he was one of Southern California's best-known and most-loved pastors.

I called him at home and asked if I could set up an appointment to talk to him about an ad. In the course of my "sales pitch" I also told him I was a Christian, and a little bit about what I had been doing in San Bernardino.

He seemed a bit preoccupied. "Why don't you come to my office and talk to me," he suggested. "I have some people with me now. Mark Buntain, our missionary from India, is here, and now isn't the best time for me to talk."

"Okay, sir, I'll do that," I said. "We have a three-line ad for . . ." and I continued trying to get him interested in an advertisement, ever the zealous salesman and eager to talk to him.

What I didn't know was that while I rambled on about costs

and sizes, the voice of the Holy Spirit was speaking very clearly to the Rev. Steelberg, regarding an open position in his church for which he had dozens of applicants. *The young man you're speaking to*, God told him, *will be your next associate pastor and director of youth.*

Suddenly Steelberg interrupted me in mid-sentence. "Excuse me, young man, but what did you say your name was?"

"Bob Weiner."

"Okay, Bob. You be at my office at nine A.M. tomorrow, and we'll talk about it then."

When I arrived at his office the next morning, he didn't even give me a chance to launch into my sales pitch. As soon as I sat down across from him he said, "I'll take your biggest ad, whatever it is."

"But don't you want to know— "

"No. I don't need to know or see anything. Just give us your biggest ad."

"Yes, sir!"

Then he got down to the business at hand. "Now, son, tell me what the Lord has been doing in your life."

I told him about the concerts we had been having, about the coffeehouse, about my plans with Bob and Tom for a cross-country trip to spread the Gospel on college campuses. I also told him about my recent beginning of a deeper walk with God through Albie Pearson, and about some of the miraculous answers to prayer I had seen.

The more I talked, the more excited he became. When I finished he said, "I want you to come down here next Sunday and tell my congregation what you've just told me."

He also invited me to go with him to a breakfast meeting of the Full Gospel Business Men's Fellowship International. I was, of course, delighted to go, especially in the company of such a distinguished Christian leader.

When we got to the breakfast, in downtown Long Beach, the place was packed. There were more than 300 men gathered in the hotel ball room. Demos Shakarian, the president of the organization, was presiding over the affair, and I was impressed and a little awed because I had heard so many good things about him and his organization. Demos Shakarian was and is a mighty man of God who has been used to bring thousands, perhaps millions, of people into the Kingdom of God.

After the breakfast, we were worshiping and praising the Lord together, when Shakarian suddenly pointed at me.

"Young man, come on up here and share your testimony with us."

Who, me? Was he talking to me? I couldn't believe it at first, but he was. With my knees knocking together, I got out of my seat and joined Demos on stage. As soon as I began speaking, all of my nervousness left me, and it was as if a special anointing of the Lord came upon me. I gave my testimony with boldness and enthusiasm, and shared my vision for reaching the youth of America for Christ.

I finished speaking to a chorus of "Praise God" and "Amen." Demos gave me a bear hug, and I went back to my seat. As soon as the meeting was over, I was surrounded by a group of men who wanted me to come share my testimony at their churches. They were excited by what I had to say, and said they knew I could bring some enthusiasm into their churches. By the time Pastor Steelberg and I were on our way home, I had enough speaking engagements lined up to last me for several months. But he reminded me that before I spoke anywhere else, I was going to share his pulpit.

So the following Sunday found me in Christian Life Church, sharing with the young people of that church what God had done in my life. Apparently I received an enthusiastic reception, and afterward the Rev. Steelberg told me, "I just want you to know that if you ever want to come and work for me, I'd be happy to have you."

"I can't tell you how much I appreciate your offer," I said. "But my friends and I are going to be taking that trip across country."

"Well, after the trip, then. Anytime you feel God telling you to come to work here, just let me know. I'll train you."

He knew that young people from all over California were

coming to know Jesus in a new and real way. He also told me he'd like to channel some of the Jesus Movement into the local churches. He would teach me everything he knew about the ministry, he promised, and I, in turn, could teach him how to be more effective in reaching young people for Jesus. "We need what you have here in this church," he concluded.

"I really do appreciate the offer," I told him, "and you can be sure I'll think about it."

Meanwhile, though, I really didn't take it too seriously. I wasn't ready to be a pastor! And how would I fit in a big-city church like this one?

On the other hand, I knew Wesley Steelberg was a mighty man of God. He could pick a youth pastor from any of the top Bible colleges or seminaries in the country. And when I, an ad salesman he had never heard of, called him up and asked him to buy an ad, he ended up offering me that position in his church! It humbled me to think about it.

Here was a man who was a leader in the World Literature Crusade, the emcee for all of Kathryn Kuhlman's miracle services, and one of David Wilkerson's best friends. He had worked closely with Oswald Smith, one of the greatest missionary pastors in history, and his own father had been the superintendent of one of the largest church denominations in America. And now he wanted to work with me—Bob Weiner!

The Rev. Steelberg didn't say a word about what God had told him. He wasn't going to put any pressure on me or insist God had said I had to come work for him. Instead, he told me later, he decided to wait on the Lord to bring it all about in His perfect timing.

As he thanked me for coming to his church to preach, he shook my hand and said, "You have yourself a great time on that trip, Bob. I'm sure the Lord will use you in a mighty way. And I'll be talking to you when you get back to California."

"Okay, well, I'll give you a call if— "

He nodded his head as he interrupted me. "Oh, I'm sure we'll be talking again!"

Chapter Three

Preparations

When September came I flew back to Chicago to get things ready for our cross-country journey and pick up the Nash. I also brought with me the page proofs for our *Sound Mind* newspaper, which we planned to distribute on campuses all across the country. Bob, Tom, and I had been praying for the Lord's direction, and we all felt God wanted us to print up 100,000 copies.

We wanted it done right, on glossy paper, with top-notch reproduction. We had gone to a lot of trouble to present the Gospel and particularly the Four Spiritual Laws in language youths could relate to. Now we needed a good printing job to give it the finishing touches. There was only one obstacle: We didn't have the money.

My dad and I got out the phone book and started looking through the Yellow Pages under *Printers*. Finally, when we worked our way all the way through the alphabet to W, there was a name Dad recognized. He thought the owner of that company was a Christian.

That was all the incentive I needed. I called the owner and made an appointment to meet with him. I wasn't sure what kind of reaction to expect, but I sat down in his office and told him we believed God wanted us to print 100,000 of these newspapers to reach the young people on university campuses, but that we didn't have any money.

"I believe God wants you to print this paper for us," I said boldly. "And if you do, I'll guarantee you that we'll pay the bill—every penny."

He stood up, and I thought for a moment he might tell me to stop wasting his time. Instead, he held out his hand to me. "I believe in you," he said. "I'll have them done within a week."

Now, once the 100,000 newspapers were printed, there was a second obstacle besides repaying the printing costs: Namely, how in the world were we going to take them with us? There was no way we could fit 100,000 newspapers into a 1919 Nash. This represented, at least, an entire truck full of newspapers.

Dad and I began praying about it, asking the Lord what to do, and He quickly gave us the solution.

The first thing we did was get a zip code directory and look up the zip codes for all the campuses we wanted to visit. Then we got from Bob Cording his list of Wheaton College alumni. It was a painstaking process, but after several hours of poring through the alumni addresses, we were able to match up the zip codes of the campuses we wanted to visit with the zip codes of Wheaton alumni.

Once we did that, Dad phoned each alumnus. He explained that Bob and Tom and I would be preaching on various college campuses along the way from Illinois to California. He also explained that we had printed up a newspaper and that we wanted to distribute it on the campuses.

Then he asked the favor: "Would you please allow us to send you several thousand copies of this newspaper? You can store them in your garage. Then, when they are in your area, they can stop by and pick them up." He closed by saying, "By the way, if you want to put them up overnight that would be fine. But there's no obligation. The main thing they need is a place to send their newspapers."

The response was overwhelmingly favorable. Just about everyone agreed to accept the newspapers from us.

A couple of days after I picked up the papers from the printer, a new wave of campus violence rocked the country. At the University of Wisconsin, a bomb placed by left-wing radicals destroyed the math building. The whole city of Madison was in a state of near-panic. People were choosing sides, and from what I read in the papers, it looked as though a war was developing. There was sure to be bloodshed. The Governor had called out the National Guard and troops were patrolling the campus.

I was praying about the situation in Madison when I felt clearly that God wanted me to go up there. I wasn't sure what I was supposed to do when I got there, but I felt that with God's help I could be a calming influence. I loaded several bundles of *Sound Mind* newspapers into the truck and back-seat of my car, and prepared to head north on the 140-mile trip to Madison.

As I was loading the papers into the car, my mother pled with me not to go.

"Mom, you don't understand," I told her. "I have to go. God has told me to go up there, and He will take care of me."

"But it's dangerous!"

"Mom, I'll be all right."

She wasn't sure she understood my radical Christianity. She had been against printing the newspapers until we had the money to pay for them, and now she was afraid I was heading into the middle of a hurricane. Besides, she wondered, how could I be sure God had really spoken to me?

"You'll have to trust me on that," I told her.

I kissed her goodbye, told her I'd be back in several days, and headed up the highway. I talked to God all the way to Madison. I asked Him to help me know what to do and say when I got there, and I thanked Him for allowing me to be one of His representatives.

When I arrived in Madison I could barely believe my eyes. Thousands of students crowded the streets. It looked like a riot searching for a place to happen. Hatred and anger hung in the air like smoke. I could actually feel it. I could feel something else, too. There was an evil presence here, and I knew Satan himself would like nothing better than to see this city erupt in a violent and bloody confrontation.

"Lord," I prayed, "I'm here. Now show me what You want me to do."

Deep in my heart I heard Him say, *Just start passing out the papers.*

So that's what I started to do. "Get a free paper here! Come get a free paper!"

Before too long, a young man with a copy of the paper in his hand came up to me. "I'm a Christian, too," he said, "and I'd like to help."

"Great! Just take a bundle of newspapers and start handing them out."

In a few minutes another Christian student came by and said that he, too, wanted to help out.

"That's terrific!" I responded. "You know, I believe that if we lift up the name of Jesus, He'll bring peace and calm into this whole situation. How about we start singing 'Amazing Grace'?"

That's what we did. As we handed out the papers we'd say, "Peace in the name of Jesus," and then we'd sing "Amazing Grace." We soon had a large gathering of Christians, all of us handing out newspapers, praying for God's peace, and singing "Amazing Grace."

Before long, representatives from seven different campus organizations were working with us, and the entire situation was growing more peaceful. People began to leave, the crowds dwindled down to nothing, and the city became sedate once again. I didn't know whether there would have been a riot without our involvement, but I did know that, with God's help, we had had something to do with restoring peace to what could have become a very explosive situation. I also learned a great lesson about unity, and especially about what Christians can do if they will lay aside their differences and work together.

Before the end of that September afternoon, a campus minister came along, a member of the Dutch Reformed Church, whom I told about the unity I had discovered. "All the Christians on campus should be getting together at least once a month," I told him. "You wouldn't believe the way everyone was cooperating out here!"

Before we said goodbye, he promised he would strive to keep that spirit of unity alive, and I felt the Lord would send a revival to the University of Wisconsin campus. I heard later that campus minister had started a prayer meeting on campus and invited all the other Christian organizations to take part. Revival did break out, and those Christians changed the atmosphere on the campus.

Meanwhile, back in Chicago, I was still awaiting the arrival of Bob Cording and Tom Rozof from California, though they wouldn't be coming for another couple of weeks. So a few days after my trip to Madison I went into Old Town on the Near North Side of Chicago to pass out some more *Sound Mind* newspapers. I wanted to do something that would make an impact on my city. After seeing what had happened in Madison I knew that with God nothing was impossible. I was to learn a second major lesson, in addition to the need for unity, in preparation for the cross-country trip.

As I walked along the streets trying to hand out my newspapers, some people would take them, others just pass me by. Meanwhile, I began to see men and women dressed in black robes who were also handing out some sort of literature. Only they weren't giving it away free; they were selling it. And they seemed to be having quite a bit of success.

Everywhere I went there were more of these people—dozens of them, all dressed exactly alike. They almost looked like actors on a break from an Alfred Hitchcock movie. I decided to check this out, so I moved in for a closer look. When I headed across the street, though, to where a group of them stood in a circle, they turned on their heels, as if by some prearranged signal, and strode off down the street. If I hadn't known better, I would almost have thought they were afraid of me.

Some passer-by had tossed one of the booklets into the trash, and I fished it out. I couldn't believe what I read. The booklet was all about how Lord Satan was the true ruler of the universe, that God was jealous and trying to strip Satan of his rightful kingdom. The booklet actually invited people to turn their lives over to Satan and begin living for him.

How ironic! Here I was, doing my best to hand out a free newspaper to point people toward eternal salvation—and these black-robed cultists were soliciting money from people to introduce them to an evil being whose only delight is seeing men and women cast into hell!

"Lord," I cried out, "where are the Christians?"

I understood for the first time how Elijah must have felt when he took on the prophets of Baal. He may not have been entirely alone, but he apparently felt like it. And right now I felt that I was up single-handedly against what must have been dozens of Satan-worshipers. Except I didn't feel much like someone who could follow in Elijah's footsteps.

Then I thought back to Tony, and the way he had prayed when the air-conditioning unit had failed and when the Hell's Angels had invaded our coffeehouse.

"In the name of Jesus," I said aloud, on my way home that night, "I bind the power of darkness, and I bind these Satan-worshipers from operating on the streets and selling their magazines here."

The next day I went back into Old Town to continue passing out my papers, and I was surprised not to find even one of the black-robed Satanists.

That day I ran into Sammy Tippitt, who was working with the evangelist Arthur Blessitt. He had come to Chicago to preach on the streets and had brought another young man with him. We began praying and working together—they helped me pass out my *Sound Mind* newspapers—and we started seeing people turn their lives over to Jesus, right there on the streets.

In the course of the day, I told them about the Satan-worshipers. We knew that there were dozens of them as opposed to only three of us. But we also knew that God was on our side.

We knelt down, there on the sidewalk, and in the name of Jesus took authority over Satan and his followers. We knew what the Scriptures said, that if any two believers agree on anything, God will grant their request. We prayed that the Satanist army would be utterly defeated and scattered.

We then continued to go about our task of telling people the good news of salvation through faith in Christ.

It wasn't until a couple of months later when I received a telephone call from Tippitt that I found out how effective our prayers had been.

"Say, do you remember those Satanists we prayed against?" he asked.

"Of course."

"Well, did you hear what happened?"

"No, what?"

"A couple of days after we prayed," he said, "the building where they were staying burned to the ground."

"It did!"

"Yes, it did. And the whole group of them left town!"

We had prayed, God had responded, and the Satanist headquarters had fallen and his army had been scattered!

A few days after taking authority over the Satanists, when I was still witnessing on the streets, I ran into a group of Christians from Moody Bible Institute. They had been trying to commence their own street ministry and wanted to talk with me about what I'd been doing.

I told them I had attended Trinity College and that I had been in California when I had come to know God in a deeper, more powerful way. They all seemed excited by what I told them, as well as by my evangelization efforts on the street. And they asked on behalf of the school if I would come to Moody and give my testimony at one of their chapel services.

So I did.

Afterward one of the students, an attractive young woman, ran up to me and grabbed both my hands. She looked as if she were about to start crying.

"You're really Bob Weiner?" she asked.

"Well, yes," I answered, wondering why that detail should provoke such emotion.

"The Bob Weiner who went to Trinity College?"

"Yes, as a matter of fact."

"Who gave my father such a hard time that he almost gave up his academic career?"

Now I gulped. I wanted to say, "Oh, no, I'm not Bob Weiner." But I knew better than to deny it.

"I probably did," I sighed. "Who's your father?"

"He was the dean of students there, and you guys gave him so much trouble that he really thought seriously about taking an early retirement."

A part of my less-than-perfect past was rising up to embarrass me.

"Your dad is really Mr. Lawhead?" I asked her.

"Yes, that's right."

"Listen, you don't know how bad I feel about the way we—er, tested the limits at Trinity. But I've changed, I've—"

"You listen." She waved her hand at me to shut me up. "You don't have to apologize. I just wanted to tell you what happened to my dad. While he was so frustrated with his job, and wondering if his life counted for anything—well, he started seeking a deeper relationship with God."

"And found what he was looking for?"

"His entire life has been changed."

To think that Mr. Lawhead's daughter was telling me that God had actually used my rebellion, as inexcusable as it was, to bless someone else! To me that was a perfect example of Romans 8:28—God making all things work together for good to bless someone who loved God, namely, Mr. Lawhead. From talking to his daughter, I found out that he now attended a church in Waukegan, Illinois. I made up my mind to attend there that very Sunday, seek him out, and tell him how sorry I was for all the grief I had caused him several years back.

When he and I finally stood face-to-face, we threw our arms around each other and both started crying.

"Brother Lawhead," I blubbered, "I just want to tell you how sorry I am. I want you to know God has touched me and I'm a changed man."

"I know you are," he cried. "So am I."

It was a moment of tremendous cleansing and release for me, and I'm sure for him, too. It was yet another step of spiritual preparation for the cross-country trip that was now only days away.

One more thing that happened before we left amazed me. I received a call from a man who said his name was Larry Zentz, and that he was calling from Trinity College.

"Bob," he said, "we feature an alumnus every quarter in the alumni newsletter, and we've heard about all what you were doing in California."

"Who is this, really?"

He didn't skip a beat. "As I was saying, we've heard about all the kids getting saved in California through your ministry, and all the things that have been happening in your life, and we'd like to feature you as Alumnus of the Quarter."

"Who put you up to this?"

Larry Zentz was finally able to convince me that, in spite of my less-than-illustrious career at Trinity, I had indeed been selected as Alumnus of the Quarter. Students who knew me then must have been surprised to see the article that ran in the alumni newsletter under the title, "A Changing Perspective." Excerpts:

> After my sophomore year at Trinity College, I joined the Air Force to fulfill my military obligation. There I had a chance to reevaluate my goals and spiritual condition. As time went on, the Lord slowly called me to a deeper walk with Him, but I decided that if I was to live completely for Him, I would have to see the power of God in action.
>
> Through a number of Christian organizations on the West Coast, I did see Jesus Christ changing lives, healing the sick mentally, physically, and spiritually. From drug addicts to successful businessmen, I saw the life-changing power of Jesus Christ through His Holy Spirit.
>
> When I experienced the fullness of the Holy

Spirit and received the dynamite that Jesus had promised, my whole life changed. . . .

In the last few months as co-director of Sound Mind Productions, a nonprofit organization in California created to present Jesus Christ to the now generation, I have seen a new coffeehouse ministry open with many results, even in the preparatory stages, as kids were coming to know Christ. . . . This is a small part of a tremendous spiritual revolution that is spreading across our country.

Admittedly, our ministry is primarily to one generation—our own, the most disturbed and disturbing generation (who need Christ) the world has ever known. . . . Christ has the answer to their personal problems as well as to the needs of the troubled world around them.

I received an excellent response to the article, especially from my former classmates. Many wanted to know what exactly had happened to get me stirred up, and it was a pleasure sharing with them, in these last days before the cross-country trip, the changes God had brought about. It was spiritual reinforcement I would need.

Chapter Four

Across America in a 1919 Nash

In late September 1970, Bob Cording and Tom Rozof arrived in Chicago. It was almost time to begin our trip. By the time we made all the arrangements and Bob took care of his previous commitments, it was the end of September. I hoped we wouldn't run into snow. This 1919 Nash wouldn't offer much in the way of protection. As a matter of fact, the old Nash had a most effective air-conditioning system—no windows except for the windshield.

But we all knew we didn't have anything to worry about. God was sending us on this trip and He would watch out for us. That didn't mean the trip would be trouble-free. In fact, we figured that with a car this old, we would be bound to have a few mechanical problems. But that, too, was in God's hands. If the car needed work at different times along the way, equal to or greater than our own mechanical ability, we'd know God was telling us to stick around for a while—that our work on that particular campus wasn't finished.

Because Bob Cording was a graduate of Wheaton College, just outside Chicago, we decided to begin our trip there. Several hundred people were on hand to wish us well, to pray for us and send us off with God's blessings. We had shoved as many of our *Sound Mind* newspapers into the back of the Nash as we possibly could, and mailed the rest of them to the previously arranged locations. We also had a guitar, an inexpensive loudspeaker, and a few changes of clothes.

We weren't setting out with much in the way of money. We had perhaps $75 among us. But we had decided to be totally dependent on God for our needs. We were not going to ask for funds but would wait for God to provide. The cash we had in our pockets—all the money we had in the world—wouldn't get us very far, but that was the way we wanted it.

We did take along a good supply of vitamins. We figured we'd probably be putting in some pretty long days on the road, and we didn't want to chance getting worn out. Our goal, after all, was to minister and preach the Gospel, and the vitamins were just an extra insurance that we would have the health to do just that.

Our first stop was Northern Illinois University, and there we began the routine that would carry us all the way to California. The first thing we always did was to find the student union building. Then we'd park in front of that, and usually the car would be enough to attract the beginnings of a curious crowd.

Tom would start playing his guitar, we'd sing perhaps three songs, and then each of us would talk for maybe five minutes, giving bits and pieces of our testimonies. It was certainly nothing fancy. It was plain and simple . . . but it worked. Of the three of us, Bob Cording was undoubtedly the most "sophisticated." He was a magazine editor and an artist, who had been a Christian for several years. As a magazine editor, he had constructed many thoughtful, logical, and eloquent defenses of the Christian faith.

As for Tom and me—we were not theologians, nor were we powerful speakers. We knew what we believed, but that was about it. But even though we were so plain and simple, our words seemed to have great effect. The Bible says that God chooses the foolish things of the world to confound the wise, (1 Corinthians 1:27), and that must have been what was going on. It wasn't even so much what we said, but that the power and anointing of God were upon us, and the kids we were talking to were convicted by the presence of God!

On our first stop we were delighted with the response we received. At least ten students accepted the Lord that first day, and that gave us encouragement and anticipation for what lay ahead. We handed out hundreds of our *Sound Mind* newspapers, left hundreds more in the student union next to the official campus newspaper, and even stuffed them into students' mailboxes. A check the following day showed that all but a few of the papers had been taken, so we left more.

From Northern Illinois University in De Kalb, we headed on to the University of Iowa, and then to Iowa State. We attracted large crowds in both places, with good results, and the local newspapers in both cities printed feature stories about our trip, even allowing us the opportunity to give a few of the reasons we were taking such a journey.

After our first few days on the road we were already starting to have a love/hate relationship with the 1919 Nash, named Barney by the former owner. It was an absolutely elegant car. We loved it, and it was great as an attention-getter. But it certainly wasn't a 1970-model state-of-the-art automobile.

In the first place, Barney's top speed was fifty miles an hour, and it would only reach that on a sharp downhill grade. It wasn't the greatest thing on fuel economy either, averaging about seven miles to the gallon for the trip. We did a lot of pushing, too. Sometimes it seemed as if we pushed it almost as far as we drove it. One reason was that we had to stay on back roads. The car wasn't fast enough to take on freeways, or even main highways.

Other times I would actually squat on the running board and reach into the engine well, trying to tune the carburetor as we drove down the road. None of us was a master mechanic when we set out, but we learned quickly—out of necessity.

Besides calling the car Barney, we also jokingly nicknamed it, "The Cloud By Day and the Pillar of Fire By Night." For just as the Children of Israel moved only when the cloud or the pillar moved, and stayed when the cloud or pillar stayed, we could move to our next destination only when the car was willing to move! And it seemed to work out just as we had thought it would. Whenever we had serious mechanical trouble, it always turned out that God had a special work for us to do in that city.

For instance, in Lawrence, Kansas, one of the fraternities invited us into their house to be the featured entertainment for a big after-dinner meeting. It was all a big joke to them, but we didn't care just as long as we were getting a chance to present the Gospel. (Not to mention the fact that we were also getting a free dinner!) We tried to take it all in a good-natured way, figuring that if they saw we were really "okay guys," they would be less apt to write us off.

When the dinner was over, and the time came for us to "entertain," the Spirit of God came down in an incredible way. We did what we always did—sang our three songs and told five-minute versions of our testimonies. But all of a sudden, a Presence came into that room. Some of the guys who had been doubled over with laughter, ridiculing us, now had tears streaming down their cheeks as they listened to us tell about what Jesus meant to us. When we asked how many of them were willing to give their lives to Jesus, at least three-quarters of them raised their hands. It was, at the time, the most incredible move of God's Spirit I had ever seen.

When it was time for us to leave, a group of the students followed us out to our car. They were so excited by what had happened that they didn't want to let us go.

"We'll quit school and come with you," one of them said.

"No, you can't do that," I said.

"Why not?" someone asked. "Before you guys came here tonight, I didn't have the slightest idea what life was all about."

"We're wasting our lives here," another student chimed in.

Finally, we were able to convince them that God wanted them to stay where they were. If they were serious about their commitment to Him they would find plenty to do for Him right there in Lawrence.

We told our newborn brothers goodbye and headed back out on the road. We wanted to be at Kansas State in

Manhattan by morning, and it was already approaching midnight.

But God had other plans.

Just as we were putting the Lawrence city limits behind us we heard a terrible noise underneath the hood: *Boom! Boom! Boom!* Something was dreadfully wrong, and then the car was coasting to a stop. I hoped I was wrong, but it sounded very much as if we had just blown a piston rod.

We pulled off to the side of the road and jumped out to assess the damage. A car that had been behind us coasted to a stop and the driver got out and came running up to us.

"What's wrong?" he shouted.

"I think we've just blown a rod!" I told him.

"I can't believe it!"

"You can't believe it?" I said. "How do you think we feel?"

"Let me explain," he said. By now a young woman was standing beside him. "This is my wife. We're both graduate students at the university."

"Oh, yeah," Bob said. "Didn't I see you on the campus yesterday?"

"Yes, we were, and that's why this is so amazing. You see, we were there yesterday and we heard what you said, and we both felt that maybe what you were saying was true."

His wife, nodding her agreement, reached over to take his hand.

"But . . . we . . . you know, I just wasn't really sure. So we prayed, even though we really didn't know God . . . and we told Him that we would follow you out of town. We told Him that if what you said is true, and we really do need to give our lives to Him, we wanted Him to cause your car to break down."

For a brief second I resisted the urge to say, "Thanks a lot!"

"Well," I said, "as you can see, our car *did* break down, so it looks like what we said *is* true."

"I'm convinced now," he said.

"So am I," echoed his wife.

And, standing there on the dark Kansas roadside in the

middle of the night, both of them accepted Christ as their Lord and Savior. Then we piled into their car. Bob stayed with them long enough to get the car fixed, while Tom and I took a bus on to Manhattan.

Once rejoined in Manhattan, we received a tremendous sign of God's care and provision for us.

We preached in one church on a Sunday night, and it was a terrific service. God was with us and many people came down to the altar to give their lives to Jesus. Now, normally, churches would take up an offering for us, or give us a love gift, even though we never asked for anything. On this particular night, however, nothing was done.

We hadn't told anyone, but the truth was, we were running out of money. We had enough left between us to buy perhaps one box of crackers and a package of sliced cheese. After the service, Tom and Bob both asked me if the church had given me anything for us.

"No," I told them gloomily, "not a thing."

Disappointment showed on their faces, but they wouldn't give in to it. "Well," Tom said, "we've got to remember that God will supply our needs." So, instead of complaining about the situation, we decided to spend time in praise and worship.

Then I remembered: "Oh, yeah, I did get one thing."

I pulled a crumpled envelope out of my back pocket. "One of the college students gave me this. He said he'd been saving his tithes for a while, and they're in here."

He had told me that God had instructed him to save his tithes. He hadn't known why until tonight, when we had appeared at his church. At that time, he said, he felt impressed that he was supposed to give the money to us.

"A college student's tithes?" Bob asked, eyeing the envelope without much in the way of enthusiasm.

"Well," teased Tom, "it might be enough to buy a couple of sodas. And I'm kind of thirsty."

"Then let's take a look!" I said in mock eagerness as I ripped the envelope open.

I pulled out a twenty-dollar bill and we all looked at each

other. Then another one, and another one. There were fifteen twenty-dollar bills in that envelope. Three hundred dollars! We were absolutely in shock.

How could we have ever doubted God's care! We danced around and yelled, and had a splendid time of worship. Then we went out and had something to eat! And no hamburgers. This time we splurged and had fried chicken.

On to Wichita State University, where we learned that the university's football team had been killed in a terrible plane crash. It was the worst tragedy to hit that city in many years, and everywhere we went it was the number-one topic of conversation. Everyone was asking why such a terrible thing had to happen, and mourning the loss of these fine young athletes who had represented their university and their city so well. Underneath all the questioning was the realization that there was something much more to life than football games, pep rallies, and bonfires. Something much, much more.

Tragedy almost always awakens a spiritual thirst in people, and that's what had happened this time. The entire city, including the university and high school campuses, were ready to hear us talk about the Lord. Now, lest anyone should misunderstand, I am not saying that God caused that football team's plane to crash just so we could preach the Gospel in Wichita. I don't believe that for a moment. In Wichita, He allowed us the privilege of bringing many good things out of what was a terrible tragedy.

Our contact in Wichita was a Presbyterian pastor, and an extremely discouraged one. His church was not growing. Revival was the farthest thing from the minds of his parishioners.

The pastor told us there was one high school in Wichita—Southeast High School—that really seemed to be having problems: racial problems, drug problems, all sorts of problems. We made an appointment with one of the administrators of the high school, an extremely capable black educator who had tried every other way to change things at Southeast without success. He made it clear up front that he was not a Christian.

"But you guys claim to have an answer, so I'll listen to you. We have drug problems and racial hatred here, and if you think you can solve all of our problems I salute you. I'll open every class I have to you."

And then he gave us his parting shot.

"You guys better have something to say!"

So for an entire day we held court at Southeast High School, talking to more than twenty classes. They would bring four or five classes together at one time. We would sit on the desk in front of the room singing our songs and giving our testimonies, while the kids would be crowding together, sitting on the floor, and listening intently to what we had to say.

By the end of the day we had seen at least one hundred and fifty kids, and possibly more, raise their hands to indicate they wanted to commit their lives to Christ. Right there in a public high school. Kids were weeping—cheerleaders and football players, black kids and white kids, all joining together and saying they wanted to try to live their lives God's way. I can't begin to explain what it was like except to say that the presence of God was so strong, it was almost for me as if I weren't there at all. It was more as if I were sitting on the outside looking in, watching God change these lives in front of me. We hadn't done anything but tell them about the love of God, and He had done the rest.

We made sure that all of these students knew we would be speaking in Faith Presbyterian Church on Sunday, and told them to invite their friends and parents.

The next day, which was Friday, we were invited into the largest junior high school in the city, where the same thing happened. Once again, we invited everyone to come worship with us on Sunday morning.

When Sunday morning came and we pulled up in front of the church, we could hardly believe what we were seeing. Cars were parked up and down the street as far as you could see, and a long line of people was crowding into the sanctuary. We were excited, but the pastor was beside himself. He had never seen anything like this in all his years there.

Once he turned the worship service over to us we did the same thing we always did. There was nothing extra-special or spectacular about it, but when the time came for me to give the invitation, at least three-quarters of the congregation came forward to give their lives to Christ. It was a moving, emotional moment for the three of us, as we watched many young students, who had been saved just days before, leading their parents down to the altar. Whole families were being transformed by this move of God's Spirit! Even the pastor's teenage son came forward, admitting that he had not been living his life for the Lord but that he wanted to change. He was so enthusiastic, he actually came running down the aisle and grabbed me. He hit my chest so hard that he gave himself a bloody nose—but he didn't care about that. He was just happy to get his life right with God.

The fire of God had been lit in that church and there was no putting it out. From there, it spread throughout the entire city. We even had a big march through downtown Wichita with young people from several Presbyterian churches to demonstrate our allegiance to Jesus Christ.

After several days there, Bob and I felt that it was time for us to move on. But six months after our trip was over Tom Rozof returned to that church to strengthen the work we had started. One of the things Tom did was to establish a Tuesday night Bible study for young people. We heard later that within six months that Bible study had grown to the point where there were more than seven hundred kids in regular attendance.

From Kansas we headed on into Colorado. By the time we motored into Greeley, winter was closing in. We were putting sheets of clear plastic on the sides of the car and taping them into place. They didn't do a great deal to keep out the cold, but they did block the wind and snow, and we were grateful for that. By this time we had been on the road for more than six weeks, and we were getting road-weary.

Many of our "contacts" had been kind enough to put us up for the night, but even then we were usually sleeping on floors, couches, or wherever we could find room to unroll a sleeping bag. We had only had hotel accommodations once, several weeks before in Kansas City.

What had happened then was that as we had prayed for a place to stay we believed God was telling us to go to the best hotel in town and ask for two rooms—free of charge.

So we went downtown, picked out the classiest-looking hotel around, and pulled our Nash up in front of the lobby. Then we went in and, with all the boldness I could muster, I told the registration clerk, "Sir, we're traveling across America reaching youth for Christ, and we would like to have two rooms, for two nights, free of charge."

You might expect me to tell you that he laughed in my face. He didn't. Instead, he went back to the wall behind him, took two keys down, and brought them over to me.

"I don't know why I'm doing this," he said, as he handed me the keys, "but here you go."

Just as I took the keys, the elderly bellhop came into the lobby.

"Is that your car out there?" he asked.

"Yes, sir!"

"Well, are you boys serious about what you say out there on your car?"

I looked outside and saw the sign we had attached to the back of the car. It read, "Chicago to California for Jesus."

"We sure are."

"Well, listen . . . the Fifth Dimension is performing right across the street at the convention center, and the concert should be over any minute. If you have any tracts or anything, I wish you'd go over there. Maybe God wants you to witness to those people when they come out of the auditorium."

It was a great idea. The Fifth Dimension was one of the most popular rock bands of 1970. At that particular time they were riding high on the charts with their hit song "One Less Bell to Answer." We knew their concert would be a sellout, and we also knew we could expect to find thousands of young people there.

We still had a couple of thousand of our *Sound Mind* newspapers stacked in the back of the car, so we grabbed as many as we could carry, and rushed over to the convention center with them. We stationed ourselves at the various exits and waited for the crowd to begin leaving.

We didn't have long to wait.

After only five or ten minutes, the doors burst open, and the people began pushing their way out into the cold night air.

"Hey, man," I approached a long-haired young man, "we've got an underground paper here. Help us spread the word!"

He took a handful eagerly and started handing them out.

"We've got some real heavy information here!" Another guy in a paisley shirt and bell-bottoms was happy to help us distribute the papers. They were disappearing as fast as we could hand them out; everybody seemed to want one.

Within fifteen minutes we had distributed them all. Back in our hotel room we thanked the Lord for His timing and for His promise that His Word will not return to Him void. We knew the newspapers would bring results, we just didn't know how quickly.

The next day we asked the desk clerk where all the hippies hung out, because we wanted to talk to them about the Lord. He sent us to a local park and, sure enough, the place was full of strangely dressed "love children."

We looked around and finally picked a group of eight or nine young men who were sitting on the ground underneath an old elm tree, engaged in a spirited discussion. If we went over and listened for a while, we were sure to get a good chance to tell them about Jesus.

But as we approached, we were surprised to hear they were already talking about the Lord.

"I'm telling you," one of them said, "Jesus is really where it's at."

"He's far out!" another one agreed.

Some of the others thought so, too. Others weren't so sure. "I don't know, man! Jesus—you know, He was cool, but my old man always said he was a Christian, and— "

"Don't think about your old man! I'm telling you, Jesus is for real!"

The conversation went on like that for some time. Bob, Tom, and I didn't interrupt, because these two guys were doing a fine job preaching the Gospel. What's more, they were on the same wavelength with the ones they were trying to reach. The three of us were outsiders, and we didn't want to spoil things.

Finally the discussion group broke up, with the Christians eliciting a promise from the others that they would at least think about what they had been hearing.

Then we walked up and introduced ourselves to the two young men who had been witnessing.

"You guys were great!" I said.

"You sure were," Tom chimed in. "How long have you been Christians?"

"You won't believe it," one of them told us, "but last night we went to the Fifth Dimension concert. . . ."

Bob and I looked at each other.

"Yeah," said the other one, "and we were higher than a kite. But when we came out of there someone handed us a copy of this paper." He reached into his back pocket and pulled out a crumpled, torn copy of our newspaper.

"We read through the article on how to get right with God," he continued, "and we prayed this prayer."

"And our lives were changed," the other one said. "We gave our hearts to Christ and gave up drugs. Now we're telling everyone who will listen about what Jesus did for us last night."

I couldn't contain myself any longer. "Praise God!" I shouted. "We wrote that paper! We passed it out last night!"

I don't remember what happened after that, exactly, except that there was a great deal of shouting and hugging and praising God. We were amazed and delighted by this demonstration of the power of the printed word.

The memory of that day would stay with me forever. And in cold, snow-swept Colorado, just thinking about it helped keep me warm. (Or at least a little less cold!)

Passing through wintry Colorado, however, I began to wonder what God wanted me to do with my life once this journey was over. For so long it seemed my life had been centered around this trip. But now that we were in the "homestretch," I began wondering what was next. I thought about Wesley Steelberg. How serious had he been about wanting me to be his youth pastor? I wasn't sure I could fit in as a pastor. I preferred to stay on the move. In any case, though, I knew my future was in God's hands.

Somewhere between Colorado Springs and Colorado City, a week or so before Thanksgiving, God showed us He had another special work for us to do. He showed us this, as usual, by allowing us to blow another piston rod on our less-than-trusty little Nash. This time none of us was much in the mood for surprises. For one thing, it was the middle of the night. We were miles from the nearest town. And, as I said, it was cold!

Nevertheless, there was nothing to do but stand alongside the highway and pray that God would send someone along soon. Our plan was that I would hitch a ride and try to bring back a mechanic, while Tom and Bob stayed with Barney.

Within a few minutes, the driver of a shiny white Cadillac saw my thumb and pulled over. A distinguished-looking middle-aged man, he lowered his window and asked what was wrong.

I told him briefly that we were traveling across country in this 1919 Nash to tell young people about Jesus Christ, but that the car had broken down and that I needed a ride to the nearest open gas station or garage.

He surveyed the situation for a second. Then he said, "Come on, I'll take you."

As soon as I got into the car I knew something was wrong with that fellow. He was driving a brand-new Cadillac and wearing expensive clothes, but his face looked troubled. More than troubled. His eyes were red, his face gray, and his mouth locked in what appeared to be a permanent frown.

Before we had driven very far, the man started pouring out his heart to me. He was a businessman, he said, on his way home from Denver with some terrible news for his family.

Several of his most recent business deals had gone sour in a big way. He had lost nearly everything he had. He was virtually having to start over. He was crushed and hurting and ready for a touch from the Lord.

I told him I was very sorry to hear about his misfortune. But, what was far more important, God cared. And if he'd give his life to Jesus he'd find the real meaning of life, which did not lie in money, power, or position.

My new friend had known Jesus once, he told me. But somewhere along the line, God had been crowded out of his life by "more important" things. He could see now, though, that he had been wrong and that there was nothing more important than a relationship with God. He knew that the Lord had sent Tom and Bob and me along at just that moment, in fact, because he needed to hear the message we were sharing.

I knew it, too, and breathed a silent prayer asking God to forgive me for my initial anger when our car had died on that lonely highway.

He pulled off the road, turned off the engine—in the cold, in the middle of the night—and I led him in a prayer surrendering his life to Christ.

As soon as he finished praying, his entire appearance changed. Color came into his face, which was now lit up by an enormous smile, even as tears rolled down his cheeks.

"I can't believe how good I feel!" he exclaimed. "You guys have to come home with me!"

He wheeled the Cadillac around on the dark highway, and we drove back to pick up Tom and Bob.

"You boys stay with me for a few days," he said, "and we'll send a mechanic out to take care of your car in the morning."

It turned out our newfound friend was a millionaire and one of the most influential men in his Colorado community. He had a beautiful home, and his wife and family welcomed us—despite the hour!—with open arms. He couldn't thank us enough for what we had done for him, and he wanted all his friends to know about the Lord, too.

The next day he even went down and made arrangements

to rent the town center. Then he placed an advertisement in the local newspaper personally inviting the entire town to come to a special meeting several nights later.

The center that night was packed. Our friend got up and told his friends and neighbors what had happened in his life, then turned the program over to us. We gave our usual presentation of singing and testimonies. And before the evening was over, many of those in attendance had accepted Christ.

But it didn't stop there.

It seemed that our host was also an influential force in state government. Every year at Thanksgiving, he told us, many friends and state government leaders, including the governor, met at a lodge in the mountains for a day of celebration. His whole family went, too. Thanksgiving was only a few days away by now, and this year he wanted us to make that trip to the mountains with him.

We were happy to do so, of course, and wound up talking about Jesus in front of some of the most powerful men and women in Colorado. The situation did not lend itself to an actual "altar call," but we did challenge those present to begin living for Jesus; and judging by the comments we received afterward, our words were well-received.

By now Barney, our car, was patched up, and we knew it was time to get back on the road. As always, we hated to leave our newfound friends, but we knew that other exciting adventures awaited us.

Those adventures, sad to say, were no longer to involve Barney so directly. We were still somewhere in Colorado, traversing one of the Rockies, when Barney's usefulness came to an end. It was freezing cold and the wind was blowing at around sixty miles an hour. Suddenly an especially strong gust of wind hit us head-on. It ripped the front and sides of the canvas roof and caused it to flap wildly. We taped it back into place and continued slowly . . . until we smelled burning rubber. A quick check of the engine showed us the rubber fan belt was rubbing against the generator—which had frozen.

We didn't know what to do, but felt for sure that we couldn't go on in Barney.

After praying on the side of that mountain road and asking God what He wanted us to do, we decided to use Bob Cording's credit card to rent a U-Haul truck. We drove Barney into the back of the truck and continued our cross-country trip.

We wound our way southward into New Mexico, then into Arizona. Everywhere we went it was the same. Some of the students were wide open. Of course, a few were hostile and challenged us on every front.

"What are you doing about the war in Vietnam?" they would demand.

"You won't end wars until you change the war that man has on the inside," I would answer. "I used to be part of the world's problem—living for myself. Now I'm part of the solution. What are you doing to stop the war?"

They couldn't answer that question. Some people considered violence and revolution the only answers for the problems facing our country in the early 1970s. Others felt what we were saying was true; they were receptive to the rest of our message.

Somewhere in Arizona I put in a call to Wesley Steelberg. He had asked me to keep in touch, to let him know how our trip was going. I told him now about hundreds of souls won to Jesus; the miraculous provisions confirming God's love and care for us; the wonderful people we had met along the way. He was as enthusiastic as I was.

Then he told me he had meant what he said several months back about my coming to work for him in Long Beach. He had an immediate opening on his staff, he said, and I was the only one who could fill it.

I still wasn't crazy about joining the staff of a church. I thought it might cost me some of the freedom the Lord had given me. But I was also willing to go wherever God wanted me to. There was much I felt I could give to Christian Life Church. And I knew there was much in the way of wisdom and knowledge I could gain through association with a man of God like Wesley Steelberg.

I told him I could start as soon as our trip was over.

Chapter Five

Now or Never

"Things are going to be different from now on."

I was standing in front of the young people of Christian Life Church. Some were listening intently, smiling, awaiting eagerly what I had to say. Others stifled yawns or picked at their fingernails.

"I hope you're paying attention," I said. "Because this is serious business. We're not about the business of *playing* church. We are going to set about to win this city for Christ. If you're not interested in doing that, then just let me know, and we'll release you from your commitment to this church."

Now I had their attention. Some looked excited. Some looked a bit frightened. Others looked appalled. But at least everyone was listening!

"I don't care who you are," I continued, "or who your parents are. Maybe your father's a deacon or your mother is the president of the missionary circle. But if you're not willing to become serious about your commitment to Christ, there is absolutely no reason for you to be taking up space in this church."

I had experienced a tremendous change in my life when Winkie Pratney had come to speak at our church. He had talked about the Lordship of Jesus—that you cannot accept Him as Savior without accepting Him as Lord. Pratney had said that you cannot play games with God, that He wants all of you or none of you. His sermon had a profound effect on me. I resolved that I would always stress the Lordship of Jesus in my own life and in my message to others. Ever since then, I have felt that Winkie Pratney is one of many "fathers" to me, along with Demos Shakarian, Wesley Steelberg, and Albie Pearson.

Now I was delivering his message on the Lordship of Jesus to the teenagers of Christian Life Church, and I wasn't at all sure how their parents would react. Still, it was a risk I had to take. In fact, I had told Wesley Steelberg that this was how I would approach the job of youth pastor, and he had agreed it was worth the risk.

I had never believed in forcing teenagers to go to church. When children are small, yes, parents should see that they are in attendance whenever the church doors are open. But there comes a time when young men and women have to make a decision about Christ for themselves. If the teens in Christian Life Church didn't want to attend worship services, they shouldn't be there. I felt it was that simple. Their boredom and cynicism would only stifle the others' enthusiasm.

No parent should ever give up on his child, of course. Rather, he should pray, pray, pray that his child would open his heart to the Lord. But I knew you cannot force a child to be a Christian.

What I wanted for Christian Life Church was a group of one-hundred-percent committed young men and women who would help turn the city of Long Beach upside-down. I was taking a calculated risk, since ninety-five percent of the teenagers could walk out the door and never set foot inside the church again.

But I was betting on these kids—and as it turned out, I was betting correctly. We lost a few, to be sure. But ninety-five percent of them stayed and pledged themselves to get right with God and give Him one hundred percent of themselves.

The new, radical commitment of our young people began

to pay off in big ways. Within the first two weeks we more than made up in new "recruits" for the kids who had decided they didn't need the church in their lives. Much of the credit for the rapid growth of our youth group had to go to Pastor Steelberg. He was not afraid to open the church to some of the new musical groups that combined contemporary music with an eternal message. When I told him I thought that we would have a dramatic revival if we invited such groups to perform in our church, he said, "Well then, let's have them here!"

Groups such as Children of the Day and Love Song began performing regularly on Sunday nights. They filled the auditorium to capacity and brought scores of teenagers to the altar.

Just before Easter 1971, I felt the Lord wanted us to hold a parade in Long Beach. Once again, Pastor Steelberg quickly agreed. All he asked was, "Do you think you can pull this thing off, Bob?"

"I know I can."

"Then do it."

I contacted all the other youth pastors in the city. We got permission to block off Long Beach Boulevard on the Saturday before Easter, and it turned out to be one of the biggest celebrations the city of Long Beach had ever seen. Thousands of kids were involved, including several marching bands. Banners everywhere proclaimed that Jesus had indeed risen from the dead.

We marched from Tenth and Long Beach Boulevards down to the park at the edge of the Pacific Ocean. Love Song was there to perform, and several prominent speakers, including the Rev. E. V. Hill, talked about the eternal life available through the resurrection of Christ. We attracted hundreds, perhaps thousands of curious onlookers, many of whom wound up giving their lives to Jesus.

The next day, Easter Sunday, our parade was given a huge write-up in the Long Beach *Press-Telegram*. The newspaper expressed amazement at such evidence of a radical allegiance to Jesus Christ.

Another time we decided to hold a march in Hollywood,

right down Sunset Boulevard. This area is a haven for all sorts of needy people—teenage runaways, prostitutes, winos, those in search of a dream they never found. We decided it was one of the best places in Los Angeles County to proclaim the love of Jesus.

Ten thousand kids were involved in that march. In addition to carrying banners proclaiming that Jesus Christ was the Lord of our lives, we carried thousands of tracts to hand out.

Somewhere along the way, I looked over and saw a member of the Hell's Angels motorcycle gang standing next to his bike, watching us go by. He was the biggest, hairiest, most tattooed man I had ever seen, and he looked utterly contemptuous of what we were doing. He wasn't the sort of person you wanted to run up to and throw your arms around. At the same time, I knew that if anyone ever needed Jesus, he did.

So I walked over to him and handed him one of our tracts.

"God loves you and I do, too," I told him.

He took the tract and began ripping it into tiny pieces. Then he threw it back in my face. He had a steely, mean look in his eye. I stood looking back at him for a minute. He was just waiting for me to do something to provoke him.

"Look, buddy," I said at last, "I don't like what you did, but I love you. Jesus loves you, too, and He wants to save you."

Then I turned around and walked away. I could hardly believe I had talked to him so forthrightly, and I wondered how he would react.

It was another fifty yards or so before I had enough nerve to turn around and see what he was doing. My heart sank. He was running after me at top speed—all 250 pounds of him! The guy's face was contorted, and he looked really angry.

"Dear God," I prayed, "I hope my heavenly home is ready for me, 'cause it looks like I'll be arriving in a couple of seconds!"

As he got close, however, I saw that tears were running down this tough hombre's cheeks. He ran up and grabbed my shoulders.

"Look," he said, "I'm sorry about what I did back there.

I've been watching all these kids, and this is what I've been looking for for ten or fifteen years. I want the love you have."

I called some of the other youth leaders together. Then the Hell's Angel joined us on his knees, right along the side of the street, and surrendered his life to Christ. I learned later that this man entered the ministry and witnessed to motorcycle groups and gangs all over the state of California.

Exciting things were certainly happening in Long Beach.

As far as I was concerned, one of the most exciting events of my first year came when Rose Russell returned to California from Kentucky for a few weeks early in the summer. We had kept in touch ever since our first meeting. I still knew she was the girl I was supposed to marry. But for some strange reason, I seemed bent on talking myself out of it. First I told myself that perhaps my emotions were getting the better of me. Then I wondered if maybe I wasn't just carried away by her looks. After all, she was a beautiful woman with soft blonde hair, clear green eyes, and a perfect smile.

Any man, seeing a woman like that for the first time, was likely to say, "That's the woman God has for me."

Of course, there was much more to our relationship than that. Rose was a deeply committed Christian. In fact, if there was one thing about her that unnerved me, it was that her faith was so deep and strong.

One time back at the coffeehouse in San Bernardino, I was late for a Bible study I was supposed to teach. When I arrived, I discovered Rose was filling in for me. Not only that, but she had the young people's undivided attention. In fact, although Rose was normally reserved, she was teaching with power and conviction. It was obvious she had a special anointing from the Lord, and, quite frankly, it scared me.

Even then I had to ask myself, "Are you sure you want to marry such a powerful girl?" I wasn't sure I could measure up and be the sort of husband she needed.

Now, as a youth pastor in Long Beach, I was still learning many things about her.

For one thing, I discovered that she had a deep devotional and prayer life. I wanted to be doing things for God, but sometimes I ran around doing things out of my own excitement and enthusiasm. It wasn't that way with her. Sometimes it was as though I was playing Martha to her Mary. While I was "troubled" about many things, Rose was content to sit at the Master's feet and learn from Him. While I was running around at ninety miles per hour trying to get things done for the youth group, Rose was willing to sit and wait on the Lord. She was as close to God as anyone I had ever known.

Rose told me once she would be willing to live her life in a tent, if that was what she thought God wanted her to do. I had the feeling she would actually feel secure and contented in that tent! She did not seen afraid to take risks, because her security was in God, not in earthly situations or circumstances.

She was exactly what I needed and wanted. Yet I was afraid of a marriage commitment.

It was Pastor Steelberg who finally decided the issue for me. He called me into his office one day near the end of the summer for a frank talk.

"Bob, how do you feel about Rose Russell?"

"Well, I—"

"Let me get to the point. Are you going to ask her to marry you, or aren't you?"

"I'm not sure if—"

But he wasn't giving me a chance to stammer my way out of this one.

"Rose has been here all summer, and she's the finest Christian young woman I've met in years. If God told you to marry her, you ought to go ahead and ask her now. If you don't want to ask her to marry you, then you'd better break up with her, because it's not fair to her to keep her dangling like this."

I knew he was right. And I also knew I wanted to spend the rest of my life with her. It was now or never.

Shortly after that, I asked Rose to marry me, and I was the happiest man in the world when she said yes.

Now that we were engaged, I couldn't wait to make Rose my wife. We set a wedding date for early September, just a little over two months away.

A few days later, Pastor Steelberg gave me the keys to the church van and asked me if I would like to call Rose and take her out to lunch. That sounded like a great idea! What's more, Rose said she was free and that she would love to go.

Perfect!

Then I looked in my wallet. It was empty. Not a single dollar in it. I reached into my pocket. I had maybe thirty-four cents. That wouldn't go very far, not even at McDonald's.

I didn't know what to do. I was too embarrassed to call Rose back and admit I didn't have any money. I was too proud to ask Pastor Steelberg for a loan. Besides, he might think I was hinting around that I needed a raise. So I climbed into the van and, for lack of a better idea, headed off down the street toward the apartment where Rose was staying, wondering how to handle the situation.

"Lord," I prayed, "what am I going to do?"

Just then a woman came running down the street, screaming and waving an apron at me. I screeched to a stop and leaned out the window so I could hear what she was saying.

"It's a snake, it's a snake!" she screamed.

I looked down the street to see if she was being chased by a snake, but saw nothing. "Where's a snake?"

"On my porch!" She was practically hysterical. "If you'll come and kill it, I'll give you ten dollars!"

Sure enough, a large snake had come out of the bushes and was slithering along on her porch. It was a simple matter to dispense with the snake, the woman paid me the ten dollars, and Rose and I had a nice little lunch. We still have a good laugh about it!

Thank You, Lord!

Within the next week or two, Rose flew back home to Kentucky to teach. Now came the hard part for me—meeting her parents.

The flight from Los Angeles to Kentucky was strange because it was too long and too short at the same time. It was too long because I was anxious to see Rose again. It was too short because I was apprehensive about meeting her parents.

Her father, Dr. Henry Russell, was a distinguished Methodist preacher, a graduate of Southern Methodist University with numerous degrees and titles to his name—and I was a radical Christian who had met the Lord in California, an honest-to-goodness Jesus person.

I had on my best suit, and my hair neatly cut, but I still wasn't sure I was the picture of the man the Russells had always envisioned for their daughter.

It turned out, of course, that all my fears were for nothing. The Russells were delightful, gracious people who loved the Lord, and we seemed to hit it off immediately. I was expecting a lot of questions along the lines of, "How do you expect to support our little girl?" but they never came. And I did my very best to convince them I was a mature, level-headed adult.

And then the time came for me to leave. I was planning on flying from Paducah to Chicago, and from Chicago back to California. But then I heard the unmistakable voice of God.

Bob, I want you to hitchhike to Chicago.

I went through all sorts of mental gyrations, trying to convince myself that it wasn't really God speaking to me. But in the end, there was no denying it and I knew that I would have to do what He was telling me. I wasn't happy about it, primarily because I didn't know how Rose's parents would react to the news. I had been trying so hard to convince them that I was a mature, responsible adult, and now I had to say, "You know, this might sound kind of strange, but I really sense that the Lord wants me to hitchhike back to Chicago."

If my news surprised Rose's parents, they didn't let on. I didn't catch them giving each other worried glances or rolling their eyes. If I felt God wanted me to hitchhike, then it was fine with them.

So, when it came time for me to leave, Rose and her mother drove me to the edge of the city of Paducah and dropped me off. It was the worst part of town—a really rundown area—and I was cringing inside, but knew I had to be obedient to the heavenly voice.

The first person to pick me up was a sixty-five-year-old

man, recently retired. He told me that he didn't normally stop for hitchhikers, but for some strange reason he just felt like giving me a ride. As we talked he admitted to me that his life was empty. He was missing something but he didn't know what it was.

I knew, and I told him. What he was missing was a personal relationship with Jesus Christ. I told him what Christ had done in my life and assured him that he would find the same peace and joy if he would surrender his life to the Lord. Within ten minutes after he had picked me up, we pulled over to the side of the road, and he was sobbing as he gave his life to Jesus.

He wasn't going much further, but that was all right with me. I was beginning to see now why God had wanted me to hitchhike. I knew that He had already picked out the people who were going to pick me up, and that the timing of my trip was in His hands.

I stood alongside the highway and stuck my thumb up.

Within twenty minutes an old green Chevrolet pulled over and the young man behind the wheel motioned for me to get in.

"Where you headed?" he asked me.

"Chicago."

"Well, I'm only going about thirty miles."

"That's fine with me."

He didn't understand that our meeting had been arranged so that I could tell him about the gift of salvation through Christ.

As we headed off down the road, we started talking about what was going on in this country, especially with regard to the unrest about the war in Vietnam.

He didn't understand it, he said, because he had just returned home from Vietnam. He had seen friends of his die over there, and it hurt him to come home to a nation that seemed, not only ungrateful, but openly hostile.

"And now I can't get a job," he said. "I've looked everywhere, and I've said I'll do anything, but there's nothing to be found."

But that wasn't the worst of it.

He had just discovered that his girlfriend was pregnant. He wanted to do the "right" thing and marry her, but he didn't know how he could ever support her. His life was a confusing, desperate mess. In other words, he was like a ripe plum ready to fall off the tree and into the Kingdom of God.

I started telling him about Jesus Christ and what a difference the Lord could make in his life. At first he was skeptical, but when I began telling him about what God had done for me, he became more interested. Then, when I told him that I was hitchhiking to Chicago specifically because I had felt that God wanted me to, he became convinced.

Before he dropped me off, he, too, had surrendered his life to Christ. He promised me that he would seek out a Bible-believing church where he and his girlfriend could get the sort of teaching and training they needed. And we prayed together that God would open the doors that had, up until now, been closed to him.

Another young man picked me up.

"I'm only going about five miles," he said. "I'm on my way to a softball game."

"So . . . what position do you play?"

"Third base."

He was wearing his uniform, with the name of a church across the front.

"Are you a Christian?" I asked him.

"Well, sort of. . . ."

And as we continued talking, he began to admit that he wasn't really living for the Lord. He went to church and played on the church team, but that was about it. Somewhere along the line he had lost the enthusiasm he had once had. We hadn't driven a couple of miles before we were praying together, and he was recommitting his life to Christ.

He was so happy, and yet tears were rolling down his cheeks.

"I'm so glad I picked you up," he told me. "Listen, would you come over to the game with me? I'd like you to talk to the rest of the guys on the team."

"That would be terrific!"

When we got to the ballpark, he began introducing me to the other players and telling them that I had changed his life. Before too long, I found myself standing on the infield dirt with all the members of both teams gathered around me listening to my testimony. I challenged them all to recommit their lives to Christ and begin living for Him. When I asked for a show of hands, nearly three-fourths of the players indicated that they wanted to turn their lives over to Jesus. Players were crying and hugging each other. It was an incredible scene! The softball game that followed was really anticlimactic.

I was having a wonderful time, of course. I had long since repented of the fact that I had been resentful when I first heard the Lord telling me to hitchhike. But at the same time, I was beginning to wonder if I would ever get to Chicago. I hadn't gone much more than one hundred miles, and I still had an awful lot of territory to cover.

Once again, I found myself standing alongside the highway with my thumb protruding.

This time a late-model luxury car wheeled off the road just beyond me. Well, this didn't look bad! At least I would be riding in style for a while.

The middle-aged, well-dressed man behind the wheel told me he was a professor at Southern Illinois University. That was good news, too, because it meant that I'd be going at least as far as Champaign, where he was going for a meeting.

As we talked I could tell that this was an extremely intelligent man. He had two Ph.D.s, and he was one of those people who strive to know everything about everything.

I asked him if he had ever accepted Christ, and he shook his head.

"No, Bob, I'm an atheist. I have some questions that no one has ever been able to answer to my satisfaction."

"What are they?"

"I'll tell you what," he said. "If you can answer them for me, I'll pull the car over right now and give my life to Christ."

I shrugged. "Okay, shoot."

The first question he asked me was, "Where did God come from?" I don't remember what the other questions were, but they were all deeply philosophical, having to do with the existence of God.

I could never even have begun to answer them on my own and I knew it. So I took a deep breath and offered a short, silent prayer: *Lord, if I ever needed wisdom I need it now. Please give me the gifts of wisdom and knowledge.* I also asked the Lord if this college professor was sincere. Was he just being argumentative, or did he really want the answers to his questions? I felt the assurance that, yes, this man was a sincere seeker, and if he got the answers he was looking for he would do just as he said he would—give his heart to the Lord right then and there.

"Well?" The professor was waiting for me to get started. I'm sure he thought I had been sitting there trying to get my thoughts together. He didn't know I was praying.

Okay, Lord, I thought. *Here goes.*

I opened my mouth to speak, and the words just came pouring out. I honestly don't remember what I said, and the words certainly weren't coming from my own understanding. I was giving him beautiful explanations of who God was and where He came from, and the professor just sat there listening, obviously enraptured.

This was, to me, an example of Jesus' words from Luke 21:12–15:

"You will be brought before kings and governors, and all on account of my name. This will result in your being witnesses to them. But make up your mind not to worry beforehand how you will defend yourselves. For I will give you words and wisdom that none of your adversaries will be able to resist or contradict" (NIV).

When I finished talking, the professor had a look of astonishment on his face.

"I've never, ever heard any answers like that!" He paused for a moment and then went on. "I'm convinced that you've answered my questions. And I'm ready to give my heart to Christ."

Once again I found myself sitting along the side of the road, praying someone into the Kingdom of God. As soon as he finished praying, his whole appearance changed. His face seemed to shine, he was so happy. He knew that all of his searching was over; all his years of casting about in the darkness for those elusive "answers" had come to an end. It was a wonderful thing to see what a difference Jesus had already made in his life.

We were still about thirty miles south of Champaign when he accepted the Lord, and that meant we were still a couple of hours away from Chicago. But my newfound friend and brother in the Lord insisted on driving me all the way to Chicago. He told me he was so grateful for his new life in Christ that taking me the rest of the way was the least he could do.

I felt a peace about it, as if this was what the Lord wanted, and the rest of the trip home was a joyous celebration. I told the professor about many of the exciting things God had done in my life, and he praised God and enjoyed the anticipation of exciting adventures to come in his own life as a Christian.

When I finally got home the first thing I did was to kneel down and thank the Lord for all the lives he had allowed me to touch. There was the sixty-five-year-old man, the boy just home from Vietnam, at least eighteen ballplayers, and a college professor. I couldn't help wondering what would have become of them if I had not been obedient to the Lord's instructions to hitchhike. It is quite possible that that might have been the last chance any of them would have had to hear the good news about Jesus Christ.

I thanked God that He had taught me, at a very early stage of my walk with Him, to be sensitive to the Holy Spirit. I was learning over and over again the truth that this is the single-most important key in witnessing to people. I know that I never want to quench or grieve the Holy Spirit. When I feel the Holy spirit say, *Stop*, I stop. When I feel Him say, *Go*, I go.

The second week of September 1971 found me back in Paducah, where Rose and I were to be married on the eleventh at Broadway Methodist Church with Rose's father performing the ceremony.

We wanted our wedding to be a celebration of God's love for us and our love for each other, and we also wanted to use it as an opportunity to witness. Even at our rehearsal dinner, we showed a movie that Bob Cording had produced called "The Son Worshippers," and invited all those present to give their lives to Christ. There were several responses.

The wedding itself was beautiful. There were at least five hundred people present—friends and relatives from all over the country. Rose was absolutely radiant in her wedding gown, and I thought to myself that heaven itself couldn't get any better than this. Later on, we heard from several of the guests who told us that our wedding ceremony had had a profound impact on their lives. Rose and I believed then, and still believe, in using every possible opportunity to tell others about Jesus. That's the most important decision a person will ever make—a now-or-never decision that will affect a person not only the rest of his life, but for all of eternity.

Chapter Six

Maranatha!

After the wedding, it was back to Long Beach and life as usual at Christian Life Church. We were very happy there, and yet we both knew that this was not to be a long-term position for us.

The church was growing every day. The youth group was doing great things around the city of Long Beach—they were a great bunch of committed Christian kids whom I loved and appreciated. And the church had just finished erecting a large new building off the San Diego Freeway. Everything was pointing toward a bright future.

But even with my brand-new office in a brand-new church, with dozens of kids getting saved, I knew that my time in Long Beach was up. I had no idea yet what God wanted me to do, but He was definitely telling me that it was time to move on.

I called a meeting with the leaders of the church, and Rose and I explained what the Lord was telling us. But the group found it hard to accept. They felt that we would be making a mistake to leave.

Even as I was sure that the Lord was telling me to go, I agreed to continue thinking and praying about the situation. I have always believed in submission to authority. The book of Acts tells how elders were appointed in every congregation of the first-century Church, and I believe that God still requires submission to authority in the twentieth century.

I also wanted to follow the biblical truth that there is wisdom in a multitude of counselors and that "every matter may be established by the testimony of two or three witnesses" (Matthew 18:16, NIV). So, even though I felt personally, and Rose did, too, that it was time for us to move on, we also felt that the Lord would have us wait and be obedient to the leadership of the church. The last thing we wanted to do was to start "shooting from the hip," and acting like a couple of Lone Rangers.

At first the church leaders were afraid that there were other reasons for my wanting to leave. They offered me a bigger salary. I told them that wasn't what I was after.

"Well," someone said, "you must have gotten a better offer from a bigger church."

"There's no other church," I said. "There's nothing except the Lord telling me that my work here has come to an end."

For three months we continued working as hard as ever at Christian Life Church. We could have acted tempestuously and said something like, "Well, God is calling us to go, and we have to go. That's all there is to it." But there was no reason to act that way: God's calling and God's timing are two different things. Rushing off before He meant us to go would mean running a risk of getting ahead of God. And that would mean big trouble!

At the end of three months, the eldership met again. This time the consensus was that I had heard from God, that He had something great for me to do, and that He would show me as I took this step of faith.

It was a time of great excitement for me, and yet I felt a little apprehensive at the same time since I didn't know what was waiting for us down the road. But the people at the church had a big service of celebration and sent us off with their blessing. It was beautiful to leave that way, being honored by the people I loved so much and with good feelings all around.

On our last Sunday morning at Christian Life Church, the wonderful missionary Hermano Pablo was preaching, and he gave an impassioned plea regarding giving for missions programs.

Now I had been telling anybody who asked that Rose and I would be "living on faith," and waiting to see what God had planned for us. But at the same time, I had managed to set aside $700—just in case this "living by faith" thing didn't work out so well.

But as Hermano Pablo was concluding his sermon I heard the Lord say something I really didn't want to hear.

I want you to give all that money you have saved to missions. Every bit of it.

"Yes, Sir." What else could I do? I wrote out a check for the entire $700 and put it in the offering plate. Now I really was going to have to live by faith! I was also going to have to tell Rose what I had done—but I knew she would understand, and she did.

That night, at the evening service, the congregation took up a love offering for me—I didn't have any idea they were going to do that—and collected well over $300.

Then the following day I went to see Dr. J. Leonard Bell, a wonderful, godly man, who was president of World Missions. Because I knew that I needed to be under authority I asked him if I could work under his leadership.

I said, "Dr. Bell, I believe that I am to be your missionary to the youth of America and the world."

He answered that he would not only serve as my spiritual "covering," but that he wanted to be the first one to contribute to my work as a missionary. He took out his checkbook and wrote me a check for $100.

Even though Rose and I both felt our calling involved reaching out to youths, we didn't know how we were supposed to go about it. And the only direction that came to us was to sit at God's feet and learn of Him. So that's what we did for the next four months. Rose did not renew her teaching job in

Seal Beach, California, which meant we had no steady source of income, and we both read the Bible, prayed, and fasted in an attempt to draw as close to Him as possible.

I honestly don't remember how we survived financially during this time, but we did. We never had any extra money in the bank, but we always had enough to buy food and pay the mortgage on our duplex, which we had bought with no down payment via the G. I. Bill. Whenever it started looking desperate, money would come in from somewhere, and always more than the amount we needed. After awhile we both got to the point where we just didn't worry about it anymore. God was indeed showing us how to live by faith.

Finally we both felt that God wanted us to fast for a week. At the end of that time we got a telephone call from Rose's father. He wanted us to come back to Paducah to hold a youth revival at Broadway Methodist Church.

"Dad," I said, "I believe that if we come revival will break out and young people from all over the city are going to be saved. It's going to turn things upside-down. Are you ready?"

"I'm ready."

I wanted to make sure my father-in-law understood what a major revival would do to his church. Revival changes things. And those who are comfortable with the way things have always been are often scared and angered by change. I knew Pastor Russell was not in that category, but I was not sure about everyone in his church, or about the staid, conservative city of Paducah.

"Well, let's not do any advertising or anything. Let's just let the Spirit draw the youth! We'll come down and hold three days of meetings and see what happens."

We decided that I would speak on Wednesday, Thursday, and Friday nights. Then, on Saturday night, I would speak at the Christian businessmen's meeting.

The first night fifty kids came. And at the end of the service, forty of them came down the aisle to commit their lives to Jesus.

The next night two hundred kids showed up, and another fifty came down the aisle to accept Jesus. These were the kids of the leaders of the community. Doctors' kids, lawyers' kids, even the city manager's daughter. It was a sight to see: my distinguished father-in-law in his collar and black robes in the water with me baptizing those excited kids. Some of them had been attending Broadway Methodist Church for years, but they had never surrendered their lives to Jesus.

On the third night of the revival, another fifty kids were saved.

The enthusiasm was incredible. These teens were absolutely on fire for God. Many of them had been set free from drugs by the power of God, and they couldn't wait to tell their friends what Jesus had done for them. One group was even using the school's mimeograph machine to print tracts to hand out to their classmates.

Rose and I felt that we needed to stay in Paducah for a while to help these kids become established in the faith. We began holding Bible study classes after school.

Then, just as we had done in Long Beach and Hollywood, we had a Jesus march through downtown Paducah. There were several hundred young people involved, and many of them were carrying banners saying things such as, "Jesus Christ is Lord," and, "I've been changed: From drugs to Jesus!" We marched right down Broadway through the heart of the city, and then turned around and marched back to Broadway Methodist Church for a baptismal service. We had invited all the parents to come and see their children being baptized into Christ, and my father-in-law and I baptized somewhere between seventy-five and one hundred teens in that one afternoon.

Every day we had kids bringing in their drugs and Ouija boards and other possessions that were keeping them from serving the Lord with all their hearts. We burned those items in bonfires. There were favorable write-ups in the local newspapers but, quite honestly, there were some problems because not everyone was able to welcome the revival with open arms. As I said before, if you want revival you had better be ready for the opposition that goes along with it.

We had been in Paducah for several weeks when it was

time for us to join a group of Jesus people from California who had been invited to come to Sweden on a "drug prevention" sweep through that country supported financially by Christians in Sweden. They had heard about the revival in California and desperately wanted the same thing for their nation, which they believed was becoming increasingly humanistic and anti-Christian. Rose and I hated to leave our newfound friends in Kentucky, but we both felt that the Lord had told us to be part of this mission trip. And so, for the next few weeks, we preached and taught in Sweden, Norway, and Denmark. We saw hundreds of lives changed in those three countries. Then one day at a large Christian conference, one of the speakers came to us and told us that he believed he had a message from God for us.

His message was that we were to return to the previous place God had been working through us and that He was going to use us in a mighty way to establish a work there that would go around the world. Rose and I both felt that this message was from God, so we started making plans for our return to Paducah.

In the few weeks we had spent there we had come to see how desperately the young people needed to know God. We had seen surveys, for instance, indicating that even in a relatively small city in middle America, some seventy-five percent of the teenagers were experimenting with drugs.

It became increasingly clear to me that God wanted me to try to buy a couple of houses across the street from Tilghman High School, which was the city's largest, and open a drug prevention center. Once that center became established, we'd turn it over to another couple, and then we'd be on our way back to California.

I knew that two houses, immediately across Washington Street from the high school, were empty, so I went to meet with the owner, asking him if he wanted to lease them.

"No," he said, "they're already leased."

"Well, how about if I buy them?"

He looked at me suspiciously. "You have that kind of money?"

I took a quick glance in the direction of heaven. "Oh, yes. I have unlimited funds."

"Hmm." I knew the gentleman was sizing me up. He had seen the California license plates on my little red sports car and my longer-than-usual hair. I wondered if he thought I was some sort of drug dealer.

"Look," he said, "if you're sure you want to buy these houses, you need to have the first $1,000 by next Friday."

"I'll have it for you."

The truth was that I didn't have any idea where I would get that first $1,000, much less the rest of the money it would take to buy these houses. But I also knew that if I was doing what God wanted me to do, and I was certain that I was, the money would be there.

I told a friend of ours about it, and he invited several of his friends to a meeting in his home to explain the situation. People were excited and generous. By the time I left his house I had $1,036 in my pockets! I took it over and gave it to the owner of the houses as earnest money. By this time I was sure he thought I was dealing in drugs to come up with that much money so fast!

But that was only the beginning. We had to have another $6,000 for the down payment and that was going to be harder to get.

And yet as word began to get around about what we were doing and why, the money started coming in. It seemed everyone was enthusiastic about the project. The newspapers were favorable, because they knew there was a drug problem in the city, and the other churches joined in, because they had seen the impact we had had on the young people—even if our presence had made some of them "nervous."

Unions gave money, civic organizations gave money—the whole city seemed to come together in support of the young people. The Holiday Inn had a warehouse full of used furniture in excellent condition. They gave all the furniture to us and we auctioned it off. That brought in a couple of thousand dollars. I was also able to sell our house in California and that money went into our fund. Other money came in from throughout the community, and in fewer than sixty days we had the $6,000 we needed for a down payment.

We promised the established churches of Paducah that we had no interest at all in starting another denomination, and we didn't. What we wanted to do was get the kids off drugs and get them saved. Then we'd send them back to the other churches.

We planned to have a library full of Christian books and records, and a Bible lab where students could come on their lunch hours or after school and listen to the Bible on audio tape. Then we wanted to have a 24-hour crisis hot line for youths, and adults too, who might find themselves in trouble.

We planned to have worship services as well, but these would be on Tuesday and Saturday nights so they would not conflict with church services.

We came up with the name Maranatha Christian Center, and we set about remodeling the two buildings. We wanted to use one building as the center and the other, a small one-bedroom house with about 900 square feet of living space, as our parsonage.

Both houses had been built in the 1930s and were badly in need of repair. There was no way we could move into either one of them in their current condition. So, until we had them fixed up, the local Holiday Inn donated a room for Rose and me where we could stay free of charge.

Once again the community rallied behind us. People pitched in to help us clean, repair, and paint, and students from Paducah area vocational schools came in and did the carpentry and electrical work for us. Before too long we had the houses in tip-top shape. We were licensed by the state of Kentucky as a drug prevention center, and the mayor of Paducah even donated a red telephone for our hot line.

We moved into the parsonage and our two counselors moved into the other building.

On the very first day our crisis hot line started ringing. We got calls all hours of the day and night, mostly from students who were strung out on drugs and who knew they needed help.

Within our first month of operation we helped more than fifty kids kick drugs for good. Most of them were teenagers from upper-middle-class families. They were not the sorts of kids you would expect to see in a back alley somewhere getting high on LSD or mainlining heroin.

One day we received a call from a young man who was freaking out on LSD. He was having a bad trip, and he needed help desperately. He managed to tell us the location of the phone booth he was calling from and we went to pick him up.

But when we got him in the car he went totally berserk. He was screaming, yelling, and trying to grab me.

I didn't know what else to do, so I took authority over him in the name of Jesus. "In the name of Jesus, you sit down and be quiet."

He did exactly as I told him, and he sat quietly the rest of the way back to our center. When we got him there we prayed for him and he was set free.

We found out quickly that prayer was the most effective means of combating drug abuse. We also found out that demonic activity was tied in very closely with such abuse. Satan and his army of evil angels were angry and upset because we were taking so many young people out of their clutches, and they often showed their anger in dramatic ways.

One girl, a very sweet young lady who was perhaps fifteen years old and who was doing her best to live for the Lord, came under demonic attack one day. She began cursing and swearing in another voice and appeared to be having uncontrollable convulsions. We carried her to the parsonage, even though she was trying the whole time to fight us and get away from us. We prayed for her there, but nothing seemed to help. Finally we sensed that the Lord was telling us to lift our hands and worship Him and thank Him that she was free according to the Word of God. That's what we did, and she was delivered instantly. Today she and her husband are in the ministry.

Another time we were praying for a young boy who was a

homosexual and who wanted to be set free from that lifestyle and those unnatural lusts. We were not getting anywhere with him and finally had to come to the conclusion that we were dealing with a demonic spirit.

I said, "In the name of Jesus I command that homosexual spirit to come out."

And, in a very high-pitched voice that was not his own, the young man said, "I'm not coming out! I've been in here since he was twelve years old and I'm not coming out!"

I said, "Well, according to the Word of God you have to come out, and in the name of Jesus I command you to leave right now. I command you, spirit of homosexuality, to come out." At that moment the boy screamed and then he fell into my arms.

That boy's voice immediately dropped about half an octave, and you could see his face taking on a more masculine appearance. It was amazing. Later that boy went into the ministry in California, with Teen Challenge. Now, I know all of this might sound strange, especially to those who have had no contact with demonic oppression, but we found out very quickly that demons are real, and they do their very best to entrap and enslave people.

We also started an early morning Bible study, and twenty-five to thirty kids would be there every morning at 7:30 to get ready for the school day. Then on Saturday nights we would show films and have musical groups perform.

Unfortunately, from the very beginning, we found that not everyone liked or appreciated what we were doing. We were saddened, though, by the fact that the first line of opposition came from some of the parents of kids we had reached. We had gotten their children off drugs and helped to get their lives straightened out, and yet some parents would call and, shouting obscenities, demand that we mind our own business. Other kids would come to our prayer meetings to report that their parents had taken away the Bibles we had given them and destroyed them. We especially had trouble from some parents who were enslaved by alcohol or drugs themselves. They seemed to resent the fact that their kids were getting straightened out. We began to think that some of these people actually wanted their children to have problems, just so they wouldn't feel so bad about their own failures in life.

It was no wonder that some of these kids had turned to drugs. They wanted to escape from a less-than-pleasant reality. And these were some of the best and brightest kids in the world once they got themselves straight. We were extremely proud of them.

You might expect that we would have had some trouble from some of the high school kids, too—especially from those who thought they were "cool," and who didn't want us coming around with our Jesus or our Bible. But the truth is we didn't have any opposition there at all. All the high school kids seemed to respect us and what we were doing. Even those who didn't agree with the Christian message knew we were there to help them out, and that we really cared about them as human beings.

That to me, along with obedience to His every directive, is another very important key to reaching people for God. If they think you see them as statistics or that your only interest in them is getting them saved, then forget it. But if they know you really and truly care for them and that your first priority is to help them, then pretty soon they're going to want to hear about your God!

At Maranatha Christian Center we had a rule that you couldn't be involved in our programs and Bible studies unless you would start going to a local church. That was another way we could make sure that our programs weren't conflicting with the local churches. But it didn't work. As hundreds of teenagers were getting saved, we were sending them into the local churches. But many of them were coming back to us with the same sad story. Namely, they weren't welcome in those churches. Remember, this was the early 1970s, and many of the churches had become very liberal and were coming down hard on "this born-again stuff" and the infilling of the Holy Spirit. Kids reported to us that they had tried to speak up in Sunday school and Bible study classes, but had been told afterward that they were not allowed to share their experiences.

I knew these kids well enough to know that they weren't troublemakers, and it bothered me immensely that people were reacting to them as if they were. Because of that opposition we eventually dropped the requirement that they had to attend another church in the area.

It was also frustrating to find a lack of concern in some surprising areas. The Paducah Ministerial Association asked me to come to their monthly meeting and tell them all about our center's drug-prevention program. I was told I would have between thirty and forty-five minutes to talk about what we were doing. Instead, the ministers spent nearly the entire meeting talking about their new recreation club.

Finally the emcee said, "Well, we have Bob Weiner here with us today, and he's going to talk about Maranatha Christian Center's drug-prevention program.

"Bob, I'm sorry, but we only have about five minutes left. So . . . could you please condense it down for us."

I was hurt! I couldn't believe they would spend an hour talking about how they could make their recreation club better, and then give me only five minutes to talk about getting kids—their kids—off drugs!

Now I knew I wasn't there to cause trouble. I was a young man, barely twenty-five years old, there to share the burden of my heart with these people, to build relationships, and get their support. But at the same time I could not sit still and pretend that everything was okay. To this day I don't know whether I was feeling my own anger or the anger of the Holy Spirit.

Whichever it was, I stood to my feet and said:

"Ladies and gentlemen, according to a newspaper survey seventy-five percent of the young people in this city are experimenting with drugs. We have a thirty-minute presentation that will show you a major solution to this problem.

"But you are apparently more interested in your recreation club than how we can minister to these kids."

Then I really went to preaching. I told them that they

needed to get out and reach their youth for Christ and to quit compromising with the world. I told them, in so many words, that they ought to be ashamed because if they were doing the job God had called them to do there wouldn't be a drug problem in Paducah. I told them that if we had these kinds of problems in the city, then all they were doing was "playing" church!

Half of the preachers got excited, and a few of them—especially most of the Baptists and one Presbyterian pastor who'd been preaching for forty or more years—were giving me some "amens," and enjoying every word of it. After I said my piece and sat down, the meeting was hastily adjourned.

As soon as the meeting was over that Presbyterian pastor came up and gave me a check for $200 to help with what we were doing. Another preacher, from the Christian Church, said, "Bob, you have to come and preach to my church about the Lordship of Jesus, and about getting out and reaching the world."

And at my first opportunity I did preach in his church. A revival broke out there and Alan Tomlin, who is now our director at the University of Texas in Austin, came to know the Lord. Alan, on the one hand, was doing drugs and living life in the fast lane, and on the other, was coming into church on Sunday morning and teaching Sunday school. But when he realized that God demands a total, one-hundred-percent commitment, he underwent a drastic transformation.

Of course not everyone felt about my speech the way this Christian Church preacher did. One minister who had been preaching for many years—and who I believe was a very godly man—came around to see me that afternoon. He wanted to give me some fatherly advice.

Putting his hand on my shoulder he said, "Bob, when you get a little older, you're going to calm down, and you're going to learn how to flow with the status quo."

"Are you telling me I'll learn how to compromise?"

"Compromise?" He looked surprised. "No, not compromise. But, you know, just learn not to make waves."

I pounded my fist into the palm of my hand. "Sir, every day

of my life, for as long as I live, I hope that I will shake the kingdom of Satan and everything that stands for him. I want to be more radical every day of my life!"

I meant it, too. You have to stand for something, or you'll fall for anything.

What God wants is a Church that has the zeal and the spirit of might upon it, not one that compromises and waters everything down and makes everything easy.

Meanwhile, back at Maranatha Christian Center, things were booming. We were packing the place out every Saturday night, and our students loved to get up and tell what the Lord was doing in their lives. There were those who had been set free from drug addiction, others who had been pulled back from the brink of suicide, and some who were finally getting along with their parents and teachers. Some of these kids, for the very first time in their lives, were facing the future hopefully.

We established a rule that no one could give a testimony if it was more than a week old. We didn't want to listen to "old" stories because God was doing remarkable new things every day. Each time we came together we had fifteen or more new testimonies the kids wanted to share. This made for some extra-long meetings, of course, but no one seemed to care. Sometimes I jokingly told them I was going to have to run them off the premises. They just didn't want to go home!

By the summer of 1973 we had decided that we wanted to reach out to surrounding communities. Christians from nearby cities had heard about the success of our programs and they wanted to implement similar programs in their towns and on their campuses. But how could they go about it?

It was finally decided that we would offer a training program. We would bring people in to stay at Maranatha Christian Center and give them the tools they needed to go back and change things in their own hometowns.

One thing we realized was that these young people needed to know how to live by faith. Everyone, including me, just trusted God for our finances. Looking back, it's really amazing how He took care of us. We never took up any offerings, and for the first three or four years I was with Maranatha I didn't draw a salary. We just believed that God would supply our needs and He did.

During our summer training program we all tithed to one another, too. If someone gave me $20, I would tithe $2 of that to someone else, and he would in turn tithe $.20 to another brother, and so on! We tithed right down to the point where it was mathematically impossible to tithe anymore.

There were days when the cupboards were just about bare, and our faith was challenged, believe me. But the Lord always came through. I remember one time in particular when we didn't have a bit of food anywhere, and it looked as if we'd just about come to the end of the tightrope.

But then we got a phone call on our hot line.

"Hey, there's a grocery store across town that's just burned down. And they want to know if you'll come in and clean it out. They're willing to give you all the food if you want it."

If we wanted it! We started jumping up and down and turning cartwheels. Then we rushed out and gathered up all the food we could carry home. Some of the cans were burnt, and the labels had come off, but we didn't mind. That only made life more interesting:

"What are we having for supper tonight?"

"I won't know until I open these cans!"

The training program was a tremendous success, and we began to get reports of exciting things going on. I also began to receive invitations to preach in other cities.

At this time, too, we organized a band called Praise that performed in churches and schools. Praise eventually recorded an album and toured all over the world, including a highly successful trip to Israel. They sang in many of the biggest churches in this country, and their anointed music has been used by the Lord in a mighty way. We heard many testimonies during the days Praise was on tour from people who had been overcome by the presence of God in the group's music.

We heard from people who would say things such as, "It wasn't so much what was said, but when you starting singing the Lord began dealing with me and I knew I had to give Him control of my life." These young kids were absolutely committed to honoring God. They asked Him to use them and anoint them when they sang, and He did.

Many fine songs were written by the members of our music groups—songs like "Blow a Trumpet in Zion." A worship tape produced by Hosannah! and featuring our Praise band leader, Randy Rothwell, is distributed around the nation.

Bob Nolte, who is now our public relations director, came to us because of Praise. Nolte had been a reporter for the Chicago *Tribune*, where he had covered Martin Luther King, Jr., the 1968 Democratic convention in Chicago, and the years of antiwar protest in America. In the early 1970s he was working as a reporter for the NBC television affiliate in Paducah. He attended a Praise concert and was so impressed by what he saw and heard there that he came back to do a feature story on what was going on at Maranatha.

Following that story he invited Rose and me to come to his house. He wanted to hear more about Jesus and about this radical Christian lifestyle we were advocating. The groundwork had already been laid, and he and his wife were ready to give their hearts to Christ. Once they had done that, Bob wanted to be involved with Maranatha in a full-time capacity.

Another man, Joseph Smith, also came to visit us in Paducah and decided to stay. He was a leading lay evangelist, a man who had held dramatic revivals around the area. He was also an executive with the GAF Corporation, a company he had been involved with for years. But when he saw what we were doing, he decided to leave all that behind and cast his lot with us. Today, he is Maranatha's vice-president.

And so, little by little, one by one, in His own timing, God sent the people we needed to guide us into the future.

And we were growing so large that we knew our future could not be confined to our two little houses on Washington Street.

We knew we had to have a bigger place when our center could barely hold the early morning Bible studies, and when we couldn't make room for much more than half the kids who wanted to come to our Tuesday and Saturday night worship services.

We began praying that the Lord would provide larger accommodations, and He did. Two Presbyterian churches in Paducah were merging, and we were asked if we wanted to buy or lease one of the buildings. This beautiful structure was situated on five acres of land right off Route 45, the main highway through town. It was too good to pass up. We leased the building and turned it into the international headquarters of Maranatha Campus Ministries. It was perfect for our purposes because it had a beautiful chapel with an auditorium that would seat around three hundred people. The grounds were also perfect for picnics and other get togethers. We felt we had room to stretch our legs.

Moving away from the high school didn't mean that we were abandoning our ministry to the students; it meant our outreach was expanding. We hadn't exactly turned Paducah into a model city, but we had definitely helped to turn things around. Tilghman High School was in much better shape than it had been when Maranatha Christian Center had first been established two years earlier, and there was a strong core of committed Christians there to keep things moving in the right direction.

They would continue to be involved in our ministry, but we knew, more and more, that God was calling us to spread His Word on the nation's college campuses.

His word to us was confirmed when several students from Kentucky's Murray State University asked if we would begin a ministry there. Jim Lewis and Debbie Anderson Caulk, both of whom had attended our leadership training program, undertook the task of getting a Maranatha ministry started on that campus. It didn't take long for word to spread, and we were invited to conduct revivals on a number of other college campuses. I would go and preach, and take a team with me, including the Praise band, to help spread the news that Jesus was alive and well. Then, once a number of students had surrendered their lives to Christ, one or two of our people would stay behind for a few weeks, and in some cases permanently, to follow up with the new believers and keep them strong in the faith.

We had seen statistics from other Christian organizations showing that it was common for many of those who made decisions for Christ not to follow through on their commitment. They'd get discouraged trying to live the Christian life and just give up.

We knew that would happen to some of the ones we had reached, too, unless we stayed behind to nourish them and encourage them. We had no intention of breezing into town, getting a bunch of people to commit their lives to Christ, and then breezing right back out of town, leaving them to wonder where they went from here. No, we would do everything we could to get them grounded and strong in the faith. I have no doubt this is one of the reasons why the overwhelming majority of the people who have been saved through Maranatha are actively serving the Lord today.

In a matter of months we built ministries at Southeast Missouri State University in Cape Girardeau, the University of Tennessee at Martin, and the University of Kentucky in Lexington.

During this time I began wondering how to help the new believers mature in the faith. They needed teaching on the basic principles of the Kingdom of God, of course, but I wanted them to get into the deeper "meat" of the Gospel as well.

We finally hit upon the idea of a Maranatha Leadership Training School.

We decided that if we could bring the best Christian leaders and teachers into Paducah for intensive training sessions, our young people would mature that much faster. So every month we brought in one teacher for six hours of instruction. We charged attendants $10 or $15 and used that to help cover costs. We also took up a love offering for the speakers. These men of God came because they were excited about what we were doing and because they wanted to share the knowledge they had with other men and women, who would then be able to go and share with others, as it says in 2 Timothy 2:2.

The Maranatha Leadership Training School was ecumenical and brought teachers in from a number of different denominations. Judson Cornwall taught us about praise and worship. DeVerne Fromke was a particular favorite of the students and returned several times. Gerald Derstine, Winkie Pratney, and Dick Mills taught our students. So did Larry Tomczak, C. J. Mahaney, Dr. J. Rodman Williams from the Melodyland School of Theology, and Dr. Charles Farrah from Oral Roberts University.

And a particular favorite of mine came to share his knowledge with us: Albie Pearson.

The school was a huge success and attracted students from all over the country. More than three hundred students came each month. To help make sure they were learning from the sessions we asked them to take notes and write reports. If you had been present at one session, you had to have your report written and turned in before you were allowed to attend the next session. We had more applications than we could handle, and we wanted to make sure that those who did come were getting maximum benefit from the sessions.

Gradually our school expanded to the point where we had to move it out of Paducah because there weren't enough hotel rooms in the city to handle all the people who wanted to attend. Eventually, the Maranatha Leadership Training School evolved into regional conferences that are held in various parts of the country each year. Every two years we have a world conference, which draws thousands of people from some sixty nations.

As the Maranatha Leadership Training School grew, so did our campus ministry.

At Southeast Missouri State University in Cape Girardeau, I had only been preaching for about ten minutes when I felt the Lord's urging to give an invitation. I wasn't anywhere near ready to give an altar call, but the prompting from the Lord was so strong that I stopped right in the middle of my sermon and gave an invitation for any who wanted to come down the aisle and give their lives to Christ. Sure enough, forty or more students came forward.

Joe Smith took them into a back room where he prayed with them and got them ready for baptism. By the time he was through with them I had given another altar call, and this time another forty students came forward.

The reaction had been such that we knew God wanted us to stay in town longer than we had planned, so we rented a storefront and began having services there. Within a matter of months we were able to buy a beautiful old house right across from the college campus and turn that into our S. E. Missouri State Campus Center.

We followed that same pattern on the other campuses we evangelized. We would find an old fraternity or sorority house that needed repair and negotiate to buy or rent it. We'd either try to raise the money to remodel the place, or we would trade our labor and materials for a break in the rent. Then, once we had done the work, we'd rent out the bedrooms to students who had become involved with our ministry. These houses would usually have a big front room, dining- and meeting-room combination, where we could seat up to two hundred students for dinners and special programs. We would also convert some of the rooms into offices as a base of operations from which to evangelize the rest of the campus, as well as the community at large.

At the University of Florida we bought a house with seventeen bedrooms and more than 7,000 square feet. We remodeled it, eventually sold it, and bought new property. At the University of South Carolina we bought an old Episcopal church, right on a corner of the campus.

Sometimes we would go into a city and establish our center before the first student had been converted. Other times we would start off meeting in a hotel or student activity center. Then, once the work had been established on campus, we would go about the task of acquiring a permanent site for our local headquarters. Today we have outreaches on one hundred and fifty university campuses around the nation, and seventy churches in some twenty countries.

When Maranatha started I merely wanted to bring the revival that had started in California to the South and Midwest regions of the United States. I wanted to come and show these kids that it wasn't dull to be a Christian—that there were contemporary Christian posters and music and things that speak to the youth culture.

As Maranatha has continued to grow and develop, the Lord has taught us a number of things about Himself and His plan for humanity. We have learned ways that every single individual can make a difference in this world, and we have learned the keys to successful Christian living and revival.

I want to share what we have learned with you.

Chapter Seven

Getting Serious with God

One thing I've learned in the more than twenty years I've been walking with the Lord is to be sensitive and obedient to His voice. If I believe God is telling me something I act on it, no matter how foolish it would make me look if I were wrong. It's like the old saying goes, everybody is somebody's fool, and I'd just as soon be foolish for God as for anybody else.

I was sitting in the window seat of an Eastern Airlines 727 one evening, heading home to Gainesville, Florida, from a speaking engagement in a Midwestern city, when an attractive young woman took the seat right next to me. There was something about her—the way she moved or dressed or looked—that was seductive. At first I wondered why she chose to sit in that seat since the aisle seat was vacant and she could have sat there, allowing us both a bit more elbow room.

But then I realized that she probably sat where she did because God had her do it. He wanted me to talk to her about something. I prayed and asked the Lord what He wanted me to say to this woman, and I heard His voice: *This woman is living in adultery. In fact, she just came from the adulterous relationship. I want you to tell her that I know about it.*

Well, there's no easy way to tell a person something like

111

that, but I figured that I would at least try to ease my way into it.

"Ma'am," I said, "I'm a Christian. As a matter of fact, I'm a minister."

She smiled and nodded, waiting for me to continue.

"And I was just wondering . . . are you a Christian?"

"Yes, I sure am." She kept smiling. "I'm a Baptist."

Hmmmm. I was beginning to wonder if I had heard the Lord correctly. Well, surely she was an ex-Baptist. She probably hadn't been to church in months.

"Oh, you are. Do you go to church now?"

She told me that she attended every Sunday and that she also taught a Sunday school class. We chatted about her class for a while, and then I sat back. Something must be wrong here. I must have really blown it.

But I could still feel that persistent pressure from the Lord. *Tell her I know about the adulterous relationship.*

I had no choice but to obey.

I cleared my throat and launched in. "Ma'am, I just have to tell you something. I've told you that I'm a Christian minister, and I want you to know that God really loves you, but His heart is broken over you."

She looked puzzled and began to interrupt me, but I continued.

"He spoke to me the moment you sat down and told me that you are living with a man who is not your husband. And I want you to know the Holy Spirit is grieved over this. He's weeping over you right now."

I didn't know what sort of reaction to expect. She could have told me I was crazy or slapped me for being so nosy or just gotten up and moved to another seat. Instead, she put her hands to her face and began sobbing.

"How did you know about this?" she cried. "All I ever needed was for someone to tell me it was wrong!"

"I'm telling you," I said, "it is wrong. And you need to put an end to this relationship."

Still sobbing, she asked, "Does this mean I'm not saved?"

I looked at her with sadness. Here was a woman who

thought she could engage in a relationship that she knew was sinful in God's eyes and still be a Christian in good standing with Him. I took out my Bible and showed her verse after verse regarding conversion and the lifestyle God expects from His children.

By the time we finished, she realized she needed to repent and come under the loving Lordship of Jesus Christ. Oh, yes, she had accepted Jesus as Savior, but never had she given her whole life to Him as Lord. We prayed together, and she committed her life to the Lord, telling Him that she wanted to live her life the way He wanted her to.

By the time our flight had landed, she was a totally different woman. Her eyes were clear and her face shone with a radiance that made her much more attractive—even though her tears had left muddy tracks through her makeup.

She told me she was going to end the illicit relationship and attempt a reconciliation with her husband, and I believed her. I knew that God had performed a miracle in her life, and I was grateful that I had obeyed His voice. If I had been more concerned with looking foolish than with obedience it is possible she would have gone on living this double life, thinking God was looking in the other direction, and been in for a rude awakening when it came time to stand before His throne.

Sadly, this is the sort of situation I encounter time and time again. People say they want to follow the Lord, but they also want to follow their own sinful pleasures. They're preaching, teaching Sunday school, serving as elders and deacons or what-have-you, and their lives are not right before God. They haven't awakened to the fact that God expects us, and has given us the power to live holy lives.

If we make a commitment to Christ, then we are saying that we choose to serve Him above all else. Only if we do that can we be truly blessed and happy in Him. Only then will we be the dominion-people He calls us to be.

I find there are seven crucial steps to follow if we are going to be true to that commitment and take the Gospel into every country in the world.

Step one is this: *We must get serious about living our lives in obedience to the commandments of Jesus Christ.* This first step may sound easy. Often, however, the Christian will miss this crucial starting point and never find his way to the life Jesus has called him to.

Are you serious about your commitment to Christ? You know that He was mighty serious about you or He never would have lived on this planet as a human being, much less suffered the agony of crucifixion. If we *are* serious we cannot look up and see Jesus hanging on the cross and still feel free to live our lives any old way we want to.

This is one of the reasons so many Christians lack power in their lives. We cannot say, "God, I want You to use me, but I also want to keep my wife *and* my girlfriend." Or, "God, please help me be a witness to my neighbors, even though I'm too tired to go to church these days." Or, "Lord, I wish You'd tell me how to deal with this situation, but, then, of course, I've got more important things to do than spend time reading the Bible."

I've been in many churches throughout this country, and you'd be surprised how few Christians I meet who are one hundred percent sold-out to God. You will see a lot of Christians at the altar on Sunday morning asking God to change them and use them. But the rest of the week, they'll be glued to the television set just like their unchurched neighbors, living a lukewarm, halfhearted, no-excitement, "counterfeit" commitment.

Jesus talks about this kind of life in Revelation 3:16. Jesus says He will spew those who are lukewarm out of His mouth. For this reason, I believe Christians are either dedicated to serving God and living under His total Lordship, or living under counterfeit conversion. There are millions of people sitting in church pews who have never really accepted Jesus as Lord, who have never really repented of all their sins and committed themselves one hundred percent to following Jesus Christ. As I have said before, they have had a counterfeit conversion. They honestly believe they're born-again Christians, but sadly, they're not.

Do you see why step one is crucial? If we want to make an impact for Christ, we have to love Him with all our hearts.

People try to save their lives a little bit here and a little bit there, and that's a big mistake. That's like the people who hold onto money that should be tithed. They think saving that bit of money every week will add up to a substantial amount. They don't realize that if they give God the ten percent income that He lovingly requires, He will take the remainder of the money and stretch it. (Anyone who has ever tried tithing can vouch for the truth of that!)

The same thing is true in a person's life. If you give yourself to God without holding anything back, He will take your life and make more out of it and you'll be a thousand times better off than you were before. The only difference is that God doesn't want just ten percent of your life. He wants it all—every bit of it!

There is no ninety-eight percent commitment or ninety-nine percent commitment. With God, it's all or nothing.

Consider the case of the rich young ruler in Luke 18. He wanted to be saved so badly he could almost taste it. And yet, when Jesus looked into his heart and saw that money was his god, He told him he would have to give it all up to be a Christian. In essence, Jesus said, "I know money is your idol, and if you want to be a follower of Mine you can't let anything be more important to you than I am. You'll have to give all your money to the poor if you want to be My disciple."

And the rich young ruler turned and walked away, because he wasn't willing to do that.

Are you willing to put Jesus first in your life? Only when you do that can you consider yourself truly a Christian, a disciple, a follower of Christ. Only when you do that will you begin to have an impact on the community in which you live.

Several years ago I was in an airport waiting for a flight when I saw an elderly gentleman I thought I recognized. I walked over and introduced myself to him and asked if he was George Gallup, the president of the Gallup Poll. He was, and we began talking about the latest trends in American thought. In the course of our conversation, I told him I was a minister.

"Well, Bob," he said, "every time we conduct a survey somewhere between fifty and sixty million Americans claim to be born again."

I nodded.

"And yet, America is going to hell faster than at any other time in her history. We have more crime, more divorce, and more social problems than ever before. Now how can almost one-third of all Americans claim to be born again and yet our country be in such bad shape?"

"Well," I said, "people in America have been taught that they can accept Jesus as fire insurance. They think they can accept Him as Savior but not make Him Lord of their lives. That's where the problem is. We have counterfeit conversion running rampant in this country. We have people who've accepted Jesus simply because they're afraid that if they don't they'll go to hell when they die. They want to go to heaven, but they have never been willing to surrender their lives totally to Jesus."

It was Mr. Gallup's turn to nod.

In Matthew 7:13–14 Jesus says: "Enter by the narrow gate; for the gate is wide, and the way is broad that leads to destruction, and many are those who enter by it. For the gate is small, and the way is narrow that leads to life, and few are those who find it."

I know that these are not easy words—especially for a world that seems to thrive on the idea of "cheap grace." But there's no such thing as cheap grace.

It's also in the seventh chapter of Matthew that Jesus says that not everyone who calls Him "Lord, Lord," will enter the Kingdom of heaven, and that's a statement that many Christians—especially those who were born in a so-called Christian nation such as the United States—should pay attention to.

Some may express their "faith" in words such as these: "Jesus, You've always been my Lord. I was born in America. My parents baptized me into the church, and I went to Sunday school every week while I was growing up." But the Lord will still be forced to say, "Depart from Me, I never knew you. You were never really Mine."

If you have accepted Jesus as Savior but have never made Him Lord of your life, I invite you to take that step right now. Bring every area of your existence into subjection to Him.

Pray this prayer right now:

Jesus, I love You and I am sorry I have hurt You and broken Your heart. I repent of my sins and my compromise. I ask that You be Lord of my life from this moment on and forevermore. I repent of walking in a spirit of deception and "counterfeit conversion." Cleanse me in Your precious blood. Come into my heart and be my Lord and Savior from this moment on. In Jesus' name. Amen.

The second step we must take if we are going to live lives that are happy and blessed in Jesus concerns moral purity. In the fifth chapter of Ephesians, Paul, writing to Christians, says:

> Walk in love, just as Christ also loved you, and gave Himself up for us, an offering and a sacrifice to God as a fragrant aroma. But do not let immorality or any impurity or greed even be named among you, as is proper among saints; and there must be no filthiness and silly talk, or coarse jesting, which are not fitting, but rather giving of thanks.
>
> For this you know with certainty, that no immoral or impure person or covetous man, who is an idolater, has an inheritance in the kingdom of Christ and God. Let no one deceive you with empty words, for because of these things the wrath of God comes upon the sons of disobedience. Therefore do not be partakers with them. Ephesians 5:2–7, NAS

Paul was writing to people who had accepted the salvation offered through the death, burial, and resurrection of Jesus Christ, and yet Paul was saying, in essence, "If you choose to live a worldly, carnal kind of life, you will not make it into heaven." Step two is this: *Moral purity is not an option for the Christian; it is a command.* Romans 12:2 says: "Do not be conformed to this world, but be transformed by the renewing of your mind, that you may prove what the will of God is, that which is good and acceptable and perfect."

Many preachers are afraid to proclaim this message because

they don't want to offend people. They're afraid of scaring people off.

But here's some surprising news: This is the message we preach on university campuses and the kids run forward by the dozens to accept Christ. Why? Because they know that what I am saying is true. They know that obedience to Christ is going to cost them everything. At the same time, they realize that by giving all they are set free. The truth always sets you free.

You can't put anything over on college students. They're too bright. They know all about easy sex and easy "highs," and they're sick and tired of that "easy" message. They want the truth, even if it's difficult, and even if it's going to hurt.

They know if you want to be a great musician you have to practice, practice, practice, and practically give your life to learning your instrument. They see the football players on their campuses working out five and six hours a day, even in the spring, when the football season is still six months away. They know that someone who wants to be an Olympic athlete trains for four, five, six years, or even longer. Any worthwhile goal takes a maximum of effort to reach.

And that's why many of them are no longer buying the message that the Christian life is easy, that all you have to do is pray one simple prayer and then it doesn't matter what you do from that time on. They are waking up to the fact that the Christian life is a constant, 24-hour-a-day submission to Christ, and I thank God for their understanding.

Now I have been asked on occasion, "How do I know if I'm really a Christian?"

My answer is this: Look at 1 John 2:3: "And by this we know that we have come to know Him, if we keep His commandments" (NAS).

If you really belong to Jesus, you will obey Him in every area of your life—starting with moral purity.

The Bible tells us that Jesus is our advocate with the Father, *if* we should sin. But somewhere along the line, most of us changed that *if* into *when*. The Bible has some very serious things to say about the man or woman who continues to practice sin after coming to Jesus, such as 1 John 3:8: "The one who practices sin is of the devil." Slipping once or twice because of weakness is one thing. Choosing to live the same old way we lived before we ever encountered Christ is another thing altogether. Romans 6:18 says that we are to be slaves of righteousness rather than slaves of sin. Does that mean we won't have any temptations? No, of course not. But 1 Corinthians 10:13 says we will never have any temptation that God hasn't given us the power to overcome. Since that's the case, is there ever any excuse for sin? No!

I am not advocating that we go back and live under the Old Testament Law. I am not suggesting a return to legalism. Rather, I am saying that under the grace of God, Jesus gives us the power to live moral and pure lives. I am calling today's Christians to live holy lives—realizing that through the blood of Jesus, the cross of Christ, and His resurrection we have been given the power to live victorious Christian lives.

All over America people think they can sin on Friday and Saturday nights, and then come to church on Sunday morning and have everything made right. Perhaps fifteen minutes before they're ready to leave for church they say a prayer such as, "Dear Jesus, please forgive me. I'm sorry. Help me not to do it anymore." But before that prayer has even left their lips they know they're going to go out and do the same thing all over again next weekend.

The writer of 1 John says that the children of God and the children of Satan are obvious because of the things they do. I tell people that Christians are not to *judge* anyone, but it is okay to be a fruit inspector. That's because the Bible says you will know them by their fruits.

Another important Scripture is:

For if after they have escaped the defilements of the world by the knowledge of the Lord and Savior Jesus Christ, they are again entangled in them and overcome, the last state has become worse for them than the first. For it would be better for them not to have known the way of righteousness, than having known it, to turn away from the holy commandment delivered to them.   2 Peter 2:20–21, NAS

119

The counterfeit, watered-down gospel we hear around us is demonic and it's breaking God's heart. If you want to play with the world, realize you cannot serve two masters. You have to make a choice.

In the New International Version of the Bible, Ephesians 5:3 says that there is not to be "even a hint of sexual immorality, or of any kind of impurity" among Christians. This doesn't just refer to the man or woman who is sexually promiscuous, but even the one who's lusting, the one who's getting himself into situations where he's doing everything but going all the way. We've got to have the guts to stand up and say, "This is wrong! This is an abomination to God!"

I do a great deal of preaching at Bible schools, and kids come up to me and tell me that they are living in immorality. They're out parking and petting and thinking that they can do everything else just as long as they don't engage in sexual intercourse. And it absolutely amazes and frightens me because these are the future preachers of America! We've got to stand up and tell our young people the truth.

When I came under the Lordship of Jesus Christ in California, I began attending a Bible-believing church. And believe it or not, I had to quit attending that church because I couldn't take the sexual pressure. I was trying my best to live a holy life, but all over that church girls were wearing short skirts and flirting with me. I figured it would have been easier to be a lothario in the church than it had been in the world! I finally had to say, "This is crazy. I'm not going to be able to make it if I stay in this church." It also made me realize I had to be cleansed of any worldliness that had been garnered in a corner of my heart from my pre-conversion days.

You see, if you have lust that dwells in your heart when you're fifteen or sixteen years old, and you don't totally repent of it and denounce it, that ugly monster is going to follow you all the days of your life. You may think you're doing well, but one of these days you'll find yourself under a lot of pressure or you'll be troubled about something—and all of a sudden that lust will have an opportunity to manifest itself. If there's no lust in your heart, however, it can't manifest itself, just as if there's no water in a cup, nothing will spill out when you shake it. If there's no tendency to sin in your heart, then when temptations come your way it's a simple matter to resist them.

If I took some dope out of my pocket and offered it to you, chances are you'd just laugh at me. Why? Because you are not tempted to take drugs. It would probably be the same if I offered you alcohol.

But if I offered heroin to a drug addict, it would be the most terrible sort of temptation. The same is true if I offered whiskey to an alcoholic. And a man who has let lust into his heart as a young man will be tempted in areas of sexual immorality. Thank God we have power over temptation!

That is why we need to start teaching our children, when they're twelve years old or even younger, about purity and holiness. We have to teach them that it's great to be holy, and break the peer pressure that causes so many of our young people to go astray.

In Maranatha Campus Ministries young people all over the country walk down the aisles at their weddings without ever having touched one another in an impure way. Many of them exchange their first kiss at the altar. Now, to the "modern" mind that may sound crazy or impractical. But I'll tell you something—it works. We probably have the fewest divorces of any Christian movement in America. You could count the number of divorces among us on the fingers of one hand—if there've been that many.

When God tells us to be holy He's not being legalistic and putting us under the Law. He tells us to be holy because He has given us the ability to do just that through the blood and cross of Jesus and the amazing grace of God.

Romans 6:14 says: "Sin shall not be master over you, for you are not under law, but under grace." Grace is the divine influence acting in you to make you pure and morally strong.

Another key to living a holy life is developing a healthy fear of God. Second Corinthians 7:1 says: "Let us cleanse ourselves from all defilement of flesh and spirit, perfecting holiness in the fear of God." People are doing their own thing, never thinking or caring about it, and they still believe that somehow everything is going to be all right come the Judgment Day. And yet there are Scriptures on top of Scriptures that talk about the holy living that is expected and required of God's people.

Suppose you are three months away from your wedding day. As you're making your wedding plans your fiancé(e) tells you that he (or she) will be totally faithful to you—364 days out of the year.

But then suppose he says to you, "But on one day a year, I'm going to be unfaithful. Now that's only one day, and the rest of the year I'm going to be a model spouse."

How would you feel about that? Chances are, you'd call off the wedding.

We wouldn't accept a wife or husband who was going to cheat on us, and neither will Jesus, the Bridegroom, accept that behavior from His Bride. When He returns to this earth, He is coming for a bride who is pure and holy—His Church. He will not receive into His Kingdom people who have other gods and other lovers, people who put other things first in their lives.

In addition to surrendering our lives totally to God, and getting ourselves morally pure, there are other areas where we need to get serious with God.

Step three is this: *Dominion people need to get serious about prayer and Bible study.* The Bible tells us to "study to shew thyself approved unto God, a workman that needeth not to be ashamed, rightly dividing the word of truth" (2 Timothy 2:15, KJV).

Some people mistakenly think that sitting in church for an hour on Sunday morning will make them strong Christians. That's wonderful, but there must be time set aside each day for prayer and for reading the Bible. Real prayer is not just presenting God with our "wish list." It is sitting in His presence, talking to Him, worshiping Him, and listening to His voice, too.

Likewise, Bible reading means a commitment of time. Some people read the Bible as if they were in a race. They zip through a chapter and say, "Well, I've done my Bible reading for the day." With this attitude, Bible reading is nothing more than a duty. They have it backward: Reading the Bible is not something done to please God; rather, it's something done to benefit us. It teaches us how to live, shows us more about God, and gives us strength when trials and temptations come our way.

When you read the Bible, take time to savor it, just as you would an elegant meal. Take time to meditate on what you're reading. And, before you begin to read, pray and ask God to help you understand and learn from what you are going to read.

In the early days of our ministry, we developed a "Fundamentals of Faith" book and had everyone study it, after which we gave a 500-question test. There were questions about the atonement, repentance, praise, worship, prayer.

We wanted our people to know the Bible, to be able to reason through Christian concepts and explain why things are as they are.

This leads directly into the next effort we must take to be dominion people. Step four is this: *We must be obedient to practice church discipline.* Too many churches are afraid to set biblical standards for their members, even though the Bible makes it clear that sin in the Body is not to be tolerated.

The Church is a Body, and we must do what we can to keep it healthy. Suppose, for instance, your arm is full of cancer. What's the most loving thing, medically speaking, to do for you? First of all, try to get it healed. The doctor uses chemotherapy and radiation, and if that works everything is fine. But if it doesn't work, he tries something else. Finally, if all else fails, there's only one thing left to do, and that's to cut that arm off before the cancer cells spread through the rest of the body. Unfortunately, this last step is being avoided in many instances in churches these days. Pastors and elders don't have the willingness to confront sin and rebellion, and it is allowed to spread through the rest of the church. Before you know it the church is dead; the Spirit has already left, and the Body is just going through the motions.

The leadership must take responsibility for discipline in the local church. For instance, in our fellowship we had a young man who became born again but didn't see anything wrong with living with his teenage girlfriend.

Following the scriptural mandate, I went to talk to him about it privately and he said, "I don't see any point in getting a little piece of paper saying we're married. I believe that in God's eyes, we are married."

I explained to him that God could not condone this sort of living arrangement, but he could not be convinced.

As the Bible commands in Matthew 18, I went and explained the situation to three of our elders. Then, when I went back to talk with him further, they came along as witnesses. Once again, I told him that what he was doing was wrong. I showed him passages from the Bible stating clearly that sexual relationships without benefit of marriage are sinful. I asked him why, if he and his girlfriend really loved each other, they didn't want to get married. I tried to approach the situation in a manner of compassion, without harshness or anger.

"Don't let yourself be deceived. We've shown you what the Bible says. This lifestyle is immoral and sensual. It is not godly."

But again, he refused to budge from his position.

At that point, I had no alternative but to take the matter before the congregation as a whole.

Explaining the situation I asked if the congregation bore witness to what he was saying. Was he right?

"No," came the answer. To him they said, "We love you, brother, but you have to repent."

"But I haven't done anything wrong."

"If that's your decision, we love you and we'll pray for you, but we can no longer walk together in fellowship, according to Scripture." As a result of our obedience, the Holy Spirit honored the church and thirty young people were saved and added to the Church the next week. God's ways are higher than our ways!

Because of the serious nature of our commitment as

Christians, such as in the examples we just discussed, we sometimes lose sight of the next step dominion-people are called to take. Step five is this: *We must learn to serve God with joy and a glad heart.* Yet even this is not without a serious side.

Deuteronomy 28:47–48 says, "Because you did not serve the Lord your God with joy and a glad heart, for the abundance of all things, therefore you shall serve your enemies whom the Lord shall send against you. . ." (NAS). The passage goes on to say that if there is no gladness in the heart, God will put an iron yoke around the neck.

I remember a service Kathryn Kuhlman was conducting at Christian Life Church in Long Beach. An older woman was sitting next to me. She was watching people all around her worship God in a joyful way, and she was seeing many of them healed of various ailments. But instead of rejoicing about what God was doing, she kept up a steady stream of moaning and complaining.

"Why doesn't God do something for me? I don't understand it, because I've been here for more than an hour now, and He hasn't done anything for me. What's going on?"

I listened to this for quite a while, until I finally had to say something. I reached over and put my arm around her.

"Listen, dear," I told her. "I think you need to quit your complaining and repent of that attitude. If you do that, I believe the Lord will move on your behalf and give you the miracle you need."

As we talked it became evident that she had a tremendous amount of bitterness in her heart. Life, she felt, had never been good to her. People were always letting her down, and so on. Finally, though, she agreed that she had to repent of that attitude that she had carried around like a yoke. I led her in a prayer of repentance, and as soon as she said, "Amen," Kathryn Kuhlman came down from the platform and walked right to where we were sitting.

The woman was using a walker and obviously couldn't walk without it. But Kathryn took her arms and pulled her to her feet, and the next thing I knew, that woman was walking all over the auditorium, praising God with tears of joy running down her cheeks. If she had remained in bondage to her old attitudes, I believe she would have spent the rest of her life wondering why God wouldn't do anything for her.

Unbuckle those yokes of wrong attitudes and serve the Lord joyfully. You may be surprised at the difference in your life!

The sixth step for dominion-people is closely related to this story: *We need to learn to exercise forgiveness.* We must, as Christians, learn to forgive those who have done us wrong. Whoever has failed you, whether it was your mother or father, your spouse, your child—even if you feel that you have failed yourself—you *must* learn to forgive. Too many Christians go around nursing grudges, not speaking to someone they feel has done them wrong, and yet they're praising God and telling Him how much they love Him.

What does the Bible say about this? If you hate your brother, whom you have seen, how can you say you love God, whom you have not seen? (1 John 4:20). If we are not willing to forgive our brothers, our own words condemn us every time we pray the Lord's Prayer. If we say, "Forgive us our debts as we forgive our debtors," and yet are unwilling to forgive our debtors, we are saying, in essence, "Don't forgive me, because I won't forgive those who have done me wrong."

Aside from doing spiritual damage, unforgiveness does physical damage as well. Doctors have found that many diseases are caused by unforgiveness and bitterness.

If you find it hard to forgive, ask God to give you the grace to do it. You can never be fully used by Him if you are going around with a heart full of unforgiveness and bitterness—no matter how well you may keep it hidden.

The steps I have been discussing in this chapter about God's expectations for His people involve serious and heart-felt introspection, but remember, "His commandments are not burdensome" (1 John 5:3). It is because of His great love for us that He desires us to walk in fellowship with Him and to reflect His holiness. God's grace is sufficient.

Chapter Eight

Learning to Hear God's Voice

A Jewish organization in Southern California was holding a big folk dance with several hundred young people in attendance. What an opportunity to talk about the Lord!

Because I am of Jewish background, I have a special love for the Jewish people, and I want to use every opportunity I can find to talk to them about Jesus.

I prayed, "Lord, let me speak to one of the key people—one of the leaders in this group."

When I walked into that synagogue, I knew right away who the leader was. He wasn't wearing a button that said, "I am the leader"; the Lord just pointed him out to me.

I walked up to him and stuck my hand out. "I'm Bob Weiner."

He took my hand reluctantly. "Well, I'm the president of this group." And then, eyeing me suspiciously, he added, "You're not one of those Jews for Jesus, are you?"

Before I even had a chance to answer, he went on.

"Listen, buddy. I don't need your Jesus!" He spat the words at me. "I'm right with the God of Abraham and Isaac and Jacob. I don't need Jesus Christ!"

And then I heard the voice of the Holy Spirit:

Tell him three things: One, that he's not right with the God of Abraham, Isaac, and Jacob; two, tell him he's living in immorality; and three, tell him that he just found out two days ago that his girlfriend is pregnant.

"I just want to tell you something," I said. "Jesus Christ, the Son of God, just spoke to me and He told me to tell you three important things."

"What was that?" He said it with a sarcastic sneer.

When I gave him the message his eyes opened wide and his mouth dropped open.

"How did you know about that?" he asked, when I told him that his girlfriend was pregnant. "We only found out about that a couple of days ago, and nobody knows but us and the doctor."

"Jesus told me."

He looked startled, as if he wanted to turn and run from me because, undoubtedly, all of his life he had been taught that no good Jew could ever believe in Jesus. But at the same time, he couldn't deny the reality of what had happened.

Perhaps he wasn't yet ready to give his life to the Lord, but God's word had definitely given me an opening.

"Tell me more about your Jesus," he said, finally.

I began telling him what the Lord had done in my life, and I could see that his interest was growing. Not only that, but several of the kids around us were listening, too. They began asking questions. Not in the hostile way you might expect, but open and interested.

Before the evening was over I had planted the seeds of the Gospel in several Jewish hearts. I knew that the Word had been given to them, and I also knew that God's Word will not return to Him void. For this reason, I expect that many of those young people are serving the Lord today, and the part I was able to play in their decisions happened because I was listening and heard the voice of God.

Now, I am no special case. I don't hear God because I have some sort of special ability—a spiritual kind of ESP. I hear God because I have learned, over the course of years of walking with Him, to listen to the Holy Spirit.

Say you have a dog that you love very much. When strangers come to the door, that dog will probably bark and growl. Why? Because he doesn't recognize the voice of the stranger. But when you come to that same door, you'll hear him whining and yipping on the other side because he knows his master has come home. He recognizes your voice, and he can't wait to see you.

Just as a dog recognizes its master's voice, the Christian must learn to recognize the voice of God.

Jesus said in John 10:4–5 that His sheep will hear His voice, but that they will not listen to the voice of a stranger. It's not that difficult to hear God's voice. All you have to do is keep the channels open—to listen for His voice and, when you have heard Him, to do what He tells you. You won't hear His voice if you don't listen for it.

Now I have never once heard God speak to me in an audible voice. I know people who claim they have had this experience, and I think it's wonderful, but it hasn't been that way with me. God speaks to the Christian in many ways, through circumstances, through the words of other Christians, and through His Word. He also speaks to us in that still, small voice that communicates with the Spirit of God in us.

I have learned, through many years of experience, that God will not talk to you if your life is not what He wants it to be. I have often heard people say something like, "I don't understand it! I have prayed and prayed and asked God for an answer to my problem. Why doesn't He say something to me?"

There are four possible answers to this question. The first is that you cannot hear God if there is unconfessed sin in your life. (See Isaiah 59:1–2.) Examine yourself, and see if there is anything standing between you and God. Perhaps it is as simple as the fact that you haven't forgiven someone who has wronged you. Or maybe it's a deeper sin that you haven't dealt with. Whatever, getting rid of it will enable you to hear His voice.

The second possible answer may be that you're simply not listening. You want God to speak to you, but He'll have to do it above all the other loud noises that are constantly running through your head. God's not going to shout over Monday Night Football to tell you what you should do. If you want His answer you have to spend time with Him, listening to Him and meditating on His Word.

The third possibility is that God has already given you the answer, but it wasn't the answer you wanted. Let's say a man has fallen in love with his secretary and he wants God to give him permission to divorce his wife. He looks at God's Word, and everything he sees teaches him that God hates divorce, that marriage is sacred, and that adulterers will be cast into the lake of fire. But even in the face of all this he still refuses to accept what the Lord is saying. "Lord," he begs, "tell me that it's all right to do what I want to do!"

This is a rather extreme example, but this sort of thing happens occasionally. You have to be willing to obey if you're going to be instructed by God.

The fourth reason you might not hear the voice of God is that He knows you are not really interested in doing His will. He is looking for people who will do what He wants, no matter what it is—and these people *do* hear His voice. Scripture puts it this way: "Today, if you hear His voice, do not harden your hearts, as when they provoked Me" (Hebrews 3:15, NAS). In other words, you can't expect God to speak to you if your heart is hard—if you haven't really made up your mind that you will respond to Him without questioning His authority over you.

In the last chapter we talked about being totally committed and sold-out to Jesus. If you have done that—truly surrendered every aspect of your life to Him—then your conscience is going to be an excellent guide for you. Now the conscience in and of itself is not infallible. Remember that the apostle Paul, before his encounter with the Lord, was following his conscience when he tortured and imprisoned members of the Church. Your mind must be renewed so the conscience can fall in line with the Word.

Perhaps your problem is not that you wonder why God doesn't talk to you, but rather that you think you're not worthy to have Him speak to you. You don't think God would talk to you so you don't expect Him to. If that's the case, look at the example of Mary. The angel Gabriel came to her and told her that she was going to give birth to a baby who would be the Son of God. She was amazed and asked how it would come about since she was a virgin. The angel said, "The Holy Spirit will come upon you. . . . For nothing will be impossible with God" (Luke 1:35, 37, NAS).

Mary may have felt that she was not worthy to be the Lord's servant—she called herself a maidservant of "lowly state"—but she was willing to receive God's Word and took part in a great miracle.

Whoever you are, the Holy Spirit will come upon you, too.

And as you begin to understand the greatness and sovereignty of God, and move out of your own power into His power, you will see some very exciting things begin to happen. Nothing is impossible to you if you are yielded to God and ready for the Holy Spirit to move in your life. If you want to hear the voice of God, pray that the Holy Spirit will open the ears of your spirit and enable you to hear.

When you begin to sense that God is speaking to you, act on it. When you feel that burning, driving force deep in your innermost being, stop and listen. If you act on the first words God speaks to you, He will begin to speak to you more and more because He knows you will be faithful. The Bible consistently teaches that those who are faithful in little things will be given the chance to be faithful in bigger things (Matthew 25:21).

You will begin to hear God's voice more clearly, and you will truly be led by the Spirit of God. It is also true that when you are obedient to God's voice, and you see the results of that obedience, your faith will be built up and you will become more and more confident.

The first time it happens you might say, "I wasn't really sure whether or not I was hearing God's voice, but I acted on it, and from the way things turned out I can see now that God was speaking to me." From that point on, you'll be able to recognize and act upon God's voice more quickly.

I mentioned earlier that God will speak to you through the Bible, His holy Word. I believe He does this in two ways. First of all, there is the general revelation of Scripture, wherein the plan of salvation is presented for all mankind. Second, I believe God will use His Word to speak to you as an individual. Remember, though, that He will never tell you to do anything that is contrary to His will as revealed in the Bible.

You see, the Bible is a living, dynamic book that speaks to believers. You will be reading the Bible and all of a sudden a particular passage will stand out. It's funny that you've never seemed to notice that verse before. Isn't it also funny how clearly it speaks to the situation you find yourself in? Didn't your heart beat faster when you read it? It seemed nearly to jump off the page at you.

Every day when you read the Bible you should look for God's special word to you. If you have been reading for an hour or so and nothing has ministered to you, keep on reading until you find that gem. It's that important.

One other way I want to mention that God may speak to you is to wake you up during the middle of the night. I have had this happen to me a number of times, and I've talked to many other people who have had the same experience. I don't know why God chooses this time to talk to His people, but it could be because that's when our minds are at peace and, therefore, most receptive.

Let's say you are awakened out of a sound sleep. You don't know why but all of a sudden you're wide awake and can't seem to get back to sleep. Well, you could get up and take a sleeping pill. Or you could ask the Lord what He wants to say to you. Perhaps He wants you to pray about a certain situation. Or maybe He is ready to give you the answer to that problem you have been praying about. If you do sense that God is speaking to you, telling you what to do, get out of bed and write it down. Even if He has given you only the first step in some complicated situation, if you demonstrate the faith to get out of bed and write that first step down, you may be surprised to find that the rest of the solution comes rapidly to you.

More than once the solution to a troublesome problem has come to me in the middle of the night. I know it can happen to any Christian who is willing to relax and listen—instead of worrying about insomnia and growing angry because you know you're going to "feel lousy in the morning." Relaxing in the presence of God is better than any amount of sleep anyway!

If you have never heard God speaking to you, this all may sound a bit outrageous. But take a look at 1 John 2:20: "You have an anointing from the Holy One, and you all know" (NAS). Then take a look at John 16:13: Jesus says, "When He, the Spirit of truth, comes, He will guide you into all the truth; for He will not speak on His own initiative, but whatever He hears, He will speak; and He will disclose to you what is to come" (NAS). So the Bible teaches that those who belong to God should be able to hear His voice through the power of the Holy Spirit. I know this isn't just an abstract theory, because I've seen it in action, time and time again.

Rose and I were in Chicago doing some work with the youth group in the church where I grew up. We were returning home from an evening service at which I had prayed for every member of the group individually. We were pulling into the driveway of my parents' house in Oak Lawn, and I was so tired and exhausted I couldn't wait to climb into a nice, soft bed.

But as we were getting out of the car, I heard the unmistakable voice of God.

There's a girl walking down the street two blocks from here. She's on drugs and she just ran away from home. I want you to go tell her about Jesus.

"Rose," I said, "you'd better get back in the car. God has something He wants us to do."

It was around 11 P.M. on a dark night. The moon in the sky was just a sliver. I squinted my eyes and looked down the street. Oh, yes, I did see someone walking down there.

We pulled out of the driveway and zoomed back down the street.

The young girl looked startled when we screeched to a stop in front of her, but I jumped out and said, "Don't be afraid! God sent me here to help you!"

Now, given a greeting like that, unless you were prepared for it, your tendency might be to turn and run in the other direction thinking a loony was after you—especially at 11 P.M.

But this girl was ready. Instead of running, she came over and threw her arms around me.

Tears were streaming down her face as she told me, "I'm on drugs and I've just run away from home and I was praying that if there was a God in heaven He should send someone to help me."

Right there on the street, Rose and I talked with her about the Lord, and she accepted Jesus Christ as her Lord and Savior. Then we took her back to my parents' house. We got her name, lined up some follow-up help for her, and took her back home.

Of course that's an amazing story. But the same thing can happen to you.

I was preaching at Western Kentucky University in Bowling Green, and I had been told by university officials that I would not be allowed to give an invitation for those attending to accept Christ. I have always tried to obey the rules and regulations of the universities at which I speak. As I was preaching I could see the students responding to what I had to say. I knew they needed to know the Lord—but remembered the rule against giving an invitation. What could I do?

Then I felt God telling me, *You open your mouth and I'll do the rest. I'll let you give an invitation* without *giving an invitation.*

"There are hundreds of you out there today who are being touched by the Holy Spirit," I said. "God is touching you right now and you want to be born again.

"Now I'm not allowed to give an invitation, because the university has asked me not to do that. But I'm wondering, if I had given an invitation, how many of you would have given your hearts to Jesus Christ?"

Some sixty or seventy kids raised their hands.

I said, "Thank God! All of you who would have given your hearts to Jesus if I had given an invitation, please see me in the back after the service."

I was able to lead every one of those kids to Jesus, and we took them across the street to a church and baptized them. Everybody was happy, including the university administration, and following that event a revival broke out on campus.

I have had the opposite sort of experience, too. Perhaps I wanted to talk to someone about the Lord, but God said no. I had no idea why. Maybe the time wasn't right and I would have done some damage instead of helping. Or maybe God was dealing with someone at that point and I would have interfered with that process. Whatever, if God says no, I'm going to be obedient.

And then there have been the times when I have been sharing with someone about the Lord and I have heard the voice of the Holy Spirit saying, *That's all I want you to share right now.*

When you are listening to God's voice you will be effective in evangelism because you will know when to share, how much to share, and when to stop sharing.

I remember another occasion during a big meeting in London. I had given the altar call, and a number of people came forward to receive Christ, including one very strangely dressed young man. He was wearing tattered clothes, was desperately thin, and didn't look too clean. In short, he was pathetic, the sort of boy you wanted to befriend and help.

But the Holy Spirit told me that we were not to touch him.

I passed this information along to the men who were helping me. "Don't touch that boy," I told them. "Don't do anything until we get everyone else taken care of." The Lord had revealed to me that the young man was under demonic oppression and that if we so much as touched him, he would cause a scene and interrupt the altar call.

One of the other Christian leaders, however, couldn't bear to see the young boy sitting there looking so lost and forlorn, so he went over and put his arm around him. Immediately, the boy started throwing his body around uncontrollably, screaming and causing a tremendous stir. There were four or five people trying to help him, but he couldn't be calmed down. Eventually, the young man was delivered from his demonic bondage and led into a new life in Jesus Christ. But, by the time we had done that, the mood of the service had changed considerably. Many people were startled by the boy's behavior and others, whom I know had been thinking about giving their lives to Christ, had had their thoughts on the subject disrupted and decided to put it off.

Yes, the young man was in need of deliverance and we did rejoice that he had been set free to start a new life in Christ. But at the same time, because the leader had not been obedient to God's voice our timing was off, and things did not go as well as they would have otherwise.

In this case, when the demons controlling that young man came in contact with the Holy Spirit residing in that Christian pastor, they couldn't stand it and began reacting violently. It was essentially the same thing that happens when a mass of hot air rumbles into a mass of cold air and you get violent thunderstorms. Satan and his demons cannot stand such close contact with the Spirit of God.

Now this Christian leader thought he was doing the right thing by putting his arm around the young man, but he wasn't. He was being led by his own feelings and emotions. This is a problem among Christians today. Too many people are acting in ways that seem right to them rather than getting any input from God in the matter.

That's one of the reasons you see so much burnout among Christian leaders. Some people think they have to do every-thing, from heading up the committee on evangelization to seeing to it that the pews are dusted once a week. If they took the time to listen to God, they would discover what He really wanted them to be doing. There might be one or two things that He has called them to do, but they're running around trying to do fifty-two other things. (I know from personal experience!)

My advice to anyone involved in that sort of whirlwind life is simply this: Don't do anything God hasn't called you to do.

Now, don't use that as a cop-out, as a reason for sitting back and letting someone else do it all. Pray about everything and make sure you're doing only that which is "born of God." God doesn't expect you to do everything, but He does expect you to do what He's calling you to do—and do it well.

But even then, don't try to do anything under your own power. Give it to God and let Him handle it.

There was a time several years ago when I learned an important lesson about all this. We had started ministries on seventeen campuses and we were in a constant spiritual battle. Every day it seemed more and more as if we were involved in a war.

I was exhausted and thinking that what I really needed was a good long vacation.

But as I was praying about things, I felt God say, *I want you to start seventeen more campus ministries within the next year.*

Then, while I was still reeling from that jolt, I heard Him say, *I want you to double your personnel, double your finances, and double the number of campuses you're on.*

Well, that wasn't exactly what I wanted to hear and I think that if one had been available, I might have hopped aboard the next boat to Ninevah, just like Jonah.

Instead, I began to complain. "Lord," I grumbled, "Your burden is heavy. You said Your yoke is easy and Your burden is light. I believe every Scripture in the Bible, but I'm having a hard time believing that one. There must be some mistake, because Your burden is heavy!"

Again, though, I could hear God speaking to me, assuring me that His Word was true.

"Well, God, I've done everything possible over the past six or seven years to get these seventeen churches started, and now You're telling me to double everything within the next year. It's more than I can handle!"

The answer that came was like a slap across my face:

Well, then, maybe you'd better look into your life and see what's wrong there, because My yoke is easy and My burden is light.

137

Then He turned me to the Scripture that says, "Whatever is born of God overcomes the world" (1 John 5:4, NAS).

And then He showed me that many of the things I was doing were not born of God. They were good things—even righteous and wonderful things. But because they were not born of God, they did not overcome the world, and they took a huge amount of effort to do.

God said to me, *Even though you're doing good things, they're some things I haven't told you to do.*

I took another look at that passage. What is it that overcomes the world? Even this—our faith. In essence, He told me that if I quit doing the things He hadn't called me to do in the first place, and if I would keep my faith level up, the things He really wanted me to do would not be a burden any longer.

I realized that I needed to spend more time in prayer and reading the Bible, getting my faith level built up. Once I had done that, I would be able to step aside and allow Him to do the work He wanted to do through me.

Now if my faith is high, that doesn't mean I won't go through trials and tribulations. Such things are a part of living on this fallen planet. But it does mean that those trials and tribulations will be overcome in joyful victory.

Unfortunately, though, I had to learn a similar lesson a couple of years ago, in a rather painful way: I had a heart attack.

It had been a really rough week. I had been on our Maranatha Satellite Prayer Network for an all-night prayer meeting, and there had been one staff meeting after another all week long. Overall it had been a tough year, and I was simply worn out.

I decided I needed a day away from it all. I'd drive over to the Atlantic coast—about a ninety-minute drive from our home in Gainesville—rent a room there, and just relax with God for the rest of the day.

As I was leaving Gainesville I could feel a dull, burning sensation in my chest but I wrote it off to heartburn and stress. When I got to the beach, the pain was still there and I could sense the Holy Spirit telling me to turn around and drive back home.

By the time I got home, I was really feeling bad, so I went straight to bed and slept until the following morning. But when I woke up, the pain was worse than ever. I called the elders and asked them to come over and pray for me, which they did. But I still didn't feel right, and so I finally asked Rose to take me to Alachua General Hospital.

At the hospital they gave me some glycerin tablets, a couple of injections of something-or-other, and put me to bed. They kept me there for ten days while they ran all sorts of tests. Finally, they told me that I had suffered a minor closure of one of my arteries.

In other words, I had suffered a heart attack.

At first I couldn't believe it. How could I have a heart attack? Perhaps that sounds a bit presumptuous, but I really couldn't understand how God would let such a thing happen—especially since all of the work I was doing was for Him. Not only *for* Him, but this time directed *by* Him.

Lying in that hospital bed, I had plenty of time for prayer and meditation, plenty of time for talking to and listening to God. And the number-one question on my mind, obviously, was, "Lord, why did this happen?"

In answer, the Lord spoke to me that I had pride in my life. I felt terrible about that, and rather defensive, too, because I felt I had never tried to exalt or promote myself. How could He then be telling me that I had pride in my life?

He had me turn to 1 Peter 5:6: "Humble yourselves therefore under the mighty hand of God, that He may exalt you at the proper time" (NAS). Well, so far so good. But then He revealed to me that the Scripture doesn't stop there. There's punctuation at the end of the verse, but it's not a period. It's a semicolon or a comma, depending upon your translation.

So what does verse 7 say? "Casting all your care upon Him, because He cares for you."

How do you humble yourself then? By casting all your care

upon God. By not thinking you're big enough to handle it all yourself.

Oh, sure, I had given God *some* of my cares. Maybe even *most* of them, but certainly not all of them. I had been carrying around a heaping mountain of worry and anxiety all by myself.

I believe God will oppose the man who is proud and who tries to work out all of his troubles by himself. I thought I was trying to do my job but I was, in reality, infringing on God's territory. It's His business to make everything work out all right—and if we'll let go and trust Him, He'll do it.

The Lord also had me take a look at Philippians 4:6 during my hospital stay. The words "Be anxious for nothing" jumped out at me. Be anxious for how much? Ninety-five percent? Ninety-eight percent? No. Be anxious for nothing at all. The passage goes on to say, "But in everything by prayer and supplication with thanksgiving let your requests be made known to God."

The following verse says that if you do that, the peace of God, which passes all understanding, will "guard your hearts."

If you don't want to have a heart attack, learn to cast your cares upon God, and His peace will protect your spiritual as well as your physical heart and keep it from being destroyed. I had allowed my anxieties to overcome me to the point where I had lost the peace of God and my heart paid for it.

Many people were praying for me during my stay in the hospital, and by the time I was discharged doctors told me everything checked out perfectly normal. That doesn't mean I'm going to go out and tempt God. It would be presumptuous for me to put as much stress on my heart as possible. I have to be careful to exercise and eat right, even though I am convinced God has healed me completely.

But one thing I have most definitely learned from all this is that whatever is happening, no matter what pressure I face or how busy a schedule I might have, I don't worry about it. I try to let God handle all the problems. I have found that is true humility.

Flowing with all of the Body of Christ — that has always been a hallmark of Maranatha. At our first World Leadership Conference in Tulsa, Demos Shakarian, founder of the Full Gospel Business Men's Fellowship International (center), prays with me and Terry Law and other Maranatha young people. It was a glorious conference!

Reaching internationals with the Gospel has a very high priority with me. I spend perhaps as much as fifty percent of my time traveling and ministering in other nations and to international students studying in the U.S. These smiling faces reflect the love of Jesus for all the nations of the world. Maranatha presently has ministries in eighteen nations, but we're working to reach all of them before Jesus comes.

Our young people are zealous to see abortion ended in our nation and often join other Christians in peaceful marches in front of abortion chambers. Many times we are able to dissuade young girls from having abortions. Some of our families have taken pregnant girls into their homes to help find alternatives to taking their babies' lives.

Even our adults love to minister on campus. Students are responsive to moms and dads who care enough to come and share Jesus on their campuses. Here, my good friend Joe Smith talks to a young man about his relationship with Jesus. Joe is vice-president of Maranatha Campus Ministries.

We believe in proclaiming the Word wherever we can! This is our ministry house at the University of Minnesota. The building buzzes with Bible studies and other Christian activities almost any hour of the day and night.

Hundreds, perhaps thousands of young people have been saved through the Maranatha outreach in the Philippines. This is a mime presentation on the streets of Manila where we meet students and share Jesus with them almost any hour of the day. A crowd always gathers when our young people begin to preach or dramatize the Gospel.

Bob Martin preaches in the streets of Manila. Bob was saved during my ministry in Murray, Kentucky, one of the first campuses on which Maranatha started a ministry. Before that, Bob was an officer in the Army serving in Vietnam. Now he is one of the "captains" in God's mighty army of preachers and prophets!

Hundreds jammed around to hear the Gospel during a summer outreach in Honduras. Students love music and respond earnestly to Maranatha evangelists who often tell testimonies of how Jesus changed their lives.

This is Barney and the boys on campus. Believe it or not, our singing and a 1919 Nash touring car were enough to bring out a crowd. We'd usually set up and start strumming in front of the student union building. The kids would flock around and before you knew it, the Holy Spirit was touching students and bringing them to Jesus. Our message was simple: Jesus loves you and He wants you to change your life.

I served in the U.S. Air Force and one of the highlights of that period in my life was a high-flying ride in a jet fighter as a prize for winning a contest held among airmen. It was exciting but not as exciting as leading young people to Jesus!

From this church in Paducah, Kentucky, scores of young people were sent to evangelize at other major university campuses in the U.S. and several campuses overseas. We outgrew our meeting space in the home across from the high school campus and were able to lease this beautiful structure on Lone Oak Road, one of the city's main streets. We had some of the most powerful speakers of the 1970s come to this church and minister to our young people.

Below: These young people are raising their hands to indicate they want to serve in full-time ministry. Many have been launched into full-time service for Jesus at our World Leadership Conferences. Other Christian leaders have told me that they have never experienced the Holy Spirit and His anointing so strongly as at a Maranatha World Conference.

It's a humble-looking place, but it was right across the street from Western Kentucky University in Bowling Green—and through its doors walked many young people who came to meetings and ended up giving their lives to Jesus. One such man, Mark Caulk, a Vietnam veteran, met the Lord here and now serves as our senior pastor at the Maranatha Church on Capitol Hill in Washington, D.C.

Our evangelism often takes us right out on the campuses where the Gospel is lovingly shared. Evangelist Rice Broocks talks with students while young people from our Maranatha Church circulate through the crowd, speaking with students who have been touched by the Holy Spirit and want to pray with someone.

From university campuses around the nation, young fiery evangelists came to pose on this special day for a photo session being held by a national Christian magazine that was doing a story in the late '70s on Maranatha. This shot was taken on the football field at Tennessee Tech University in Cookeville.

Open-air street evangelism is another staple in Maranatha. Here, Bob Nolte shares Jesus with two English college students in Oxford where we started an outreach in 1980. Bob later became our director of ministry relations and television producer. He and his family were saved in those early Paducah revival fires!

Above: It may not look like the 1980 s, but in the early Jesus-Revolution days of the '70s, such artwork was cutting-edge. We passed this newspaper out to thousands of young people across the U.S. and got reports of kids being saved as a result. More than a decade later, Maranatha's *Forerunner* newspaper, edited by Lee Grady, would fan across the U.S. and many countries of the world to plant seeds of the Gospel and victorious living among thousands of hungry readers.

Rose is the most powerful woman of God that I know. She has been an example wife and a prophet who has helped keep Maranatha right on target with what God wants for the ministry. This is Rose on the set of the "Forerunner" TV show of which she has become a major segment, teaching America's Christian heritage and ministering prophetically to viewers.

One of our most beautiful centers was at the University of Florida. It was across from the campus and drew quite a bit of attention. We had another handsome fraternity house-turned-chapel at Auburn University. We were given a city beautification award for that stately mansion. God was given much honor for the beauty of these early Maranatha centers.

This is my terrific family. That's Stephanie Elizabeth on the left (she plays
the harp) and little Evangeline below
my wife, Rose. John David is my star
soccer player and a preacher of the
Word. Since this picture was taken, a
new little prophetess has come into
the family — Catherine Grace.

One evening after a service in North
Carolina, a young Christian couple,
Jimmy and Jan Chamblin, came to me
with a special prayer request. They
wanted desperately to have a child,
but doctors had said it was impossible.
We prayed together, and I didn't hear
from them until a couple of years later
when they were passing through Florida. "We just wanted to show you
the result of that prayer," said Jimmy,
and out of the car bounced their little
son Joshua!

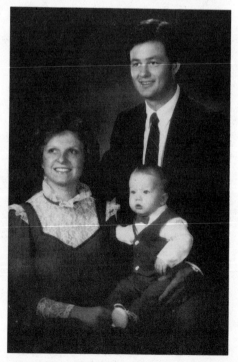

Chapter Nine

Yes, You Can Change the World

It happened in Knoxville, near the campus of the University of Tennessee.

I was driving along the street one evening when a huge sign caught my attention.

In bright colorful letters the sign announced, *Grand Opening 9 P.M.* Tonight. Knoxville was about to get another bar. Other signs in the windows of the building announced the evening's drink specials and invited university students to come in and get acquainted.

"Just what they need," I mumbled, "another place to get hooked on booze."

As soon as I could, I pulled over to the side of the road.

"Lord," I prayed, "the last thing this city needs is another bar. All these people here—all these students at the University of Tennessee—they need You, and not another place to drink.

"I'm asking You, Lord, to shut this bar down before it has a chance to ruin anyone's life. Please don't let this bar open."

Having left the situation in God's hands, I forgot about it until the next afternoon when business took me back down the same street. When I got to the bar, the Grand Opening sign was gone. In its place was a new sign, just as prominent, reading, *Out of Business.*

Even though I had seen God perform many miracles before, I could hardly believe my eyes. That had to be the fastest trip from opening day to closing day in the history of business.

From the information we could get, the bar owner gave his life to Christ, closed his bar, and began working as a youth leader for a Baptist church in Knoxville.

Some people might think that it was an amazing coincidence that this happened on the very same day I prayed and asked God not to let the bar open. They might also call it a coincidence when I tell them it was only a short time after I prayed that the young man closed the bar. But people who talk about coincidences don't know the power of God, nor do they understand the power that Christians possess as children of God.

It's interesting that my prayer was in a negative form, "Please don't let this bar open," and that God answered it in a positive form. One terrific way to keep the bar from opening was to have the owner become born again. And today, think of the hundreds of young lives that man has touched for Jesus.

And even that is not the end of the story.

Back in 1983 I was preaching at Calvary Church in Singapore and I told the story of the Knoxville bar. After the service, some of the members started telling me about a notorious bar that was right next door to the church building. It had been there for twenty-five years and had been a constant source of frustration for the members of the church.

It was a place where prostitutes liked to hang out and, even though the church worked hard to rescue those who had been entrapped by the bar, the bar seemed just as intent to find new victims to drag into hell. All sorts of evil things were going on there. The members of the church had worked and prayed and asked God to do something about the bar, to close it down.

"Bob," someone asked, "would you pray with us that the

bar will close down? We believe God has given you the faith to agree with us in prayer to close the bar."

I led the congregation in prayer that God would close that bar, just as He had the bar in Tennessee.

The next day the bar was still doing business as usual. And even a week later, when I had to fly back to the States, nothing out of the ordinary had happened.

But I knew that something exciting was just around the corner.

It was several years before I got back to Singapore. A pastor met me at the airport and on our way into the city he told me excitedly about his church's Bible school where dozens of men and women were studying to become preachers and teachers of God's Word.

I was excited, too, and told him I couldn't wait to see it.

Well, he said, why didn't we go right over there and take a tour of the facilities.

And do you know what? The Bible school was in the same building that had once housed that center of drunkenness and prostitution! The bar had closed down after doing a booming business for some twenty-five years.

The church leased the building and today, in addition to the Bible school, ten different Chinese worship services are held there every week. The church's library is also located in that building.

Meanwhile, the church has experienced phenomenal growth in these past four years. Its membership has increased from around one thousand to nearly five thousand.

If we, as Christians, are going to win this world for Christ, then there are certain things we must do. I have already talked about proving we are serious with God by surrendering our lives completely to Him. And I have talked about the importance of learning to hear and obey the voice of God. It is just as important that we learn to use the authority God has given us as His children—in other words, take dominion over this planet.

It is amazing to me that so many Christians refuse to believe what the Bible says. We claim to believe it, but when it gets right down to basics, we are proving constantly that we don't.

Jesus said: "I will give you the keys of the kingdom of heaven; and whatever you shall bind on earth shall be bound in heaven, and whatever you shall loose on earth shall be loosed in heaven" (Matthew 16:19, NAS). Why don't we believe that? He also said that all authority has been given to Him (Matthew 28:18). How much authority? *All* authority. In essence, He told us, "I have rendered Satan powerless. I have made an open show of Satan's kingdom. Now, dear Church, go in My Name, in My authority, and preach the Gospel."

We sometimes act as if we think maybe He was fooling us. But history is always repeating itself, and time and time again I have seen what will happen when people really learn how to believe.

In Los Angeles I told about the two bars closing down. After the service, a college student came up and asked if we could talk for a few minutes. He was excited by what he had heard and wanted to know if I thought it would "work" for him.

"Are you living for Jesus?"

"Yes, I am."

"In that case, yes, it will work for you, too."

He went on to explain that there was a pornographic bookstore in his neighborhood. He walked past it on his way home from school and, judging by the sorts of things in the windows, this store was peddling the worst kind of filth and sleaze.

"Well, I'm going down there," he told me, "and I'm going to lay hands on that building and tell it to close down in the name of Jesus."

That's exactly what he did, and that young man through his faith in God was able to do what the PTA and all the churches in the neighborhood had been unable to do through political pressure. He closed that bookstore down, and it happened within a couple of months.

Can you imagine what would happen if every Christian in the world had that kind of faith and took that kind of action?

We could put all the pornographers out of business practically overnight! Think of what we could do to stop the flow of drugs into this country. Imagine Christians banding together to stop the crime in their cities—even taking authority over organized crime in the name of Jesus.

Everyone remembers what happened a few years ago when the United States sent Marines into Grenada and threw the Cuban and Russian "advisors" out of that little country.

Suppose we had told the citizens there, "Okay, now you're free from Communist infiltration and you can have democracy." And suppose they had answered us, "Well, we know the Americans have come, but we don't really believe we have liberty. Oh, yes, we know that when Jesus comes again we will be set free, but until then we are going to be overrun by the Communists."

Then, eventually, through their apathy and lack of faith, Communism would return to that island, and the people would end up under the thumb of a Cuban-backed dictatorship.

Well, that's the sort of thing that's going on in the Church of Jesus Christ today. Through apathy and a lot of bad eschatology we have become fatalists who believe that everything is going to get worse and worse until Jesus finally comes back. But the truth is that God has given His people dominion over this planet, and He expects us to work to see goodness and righteousness established!

In Isaiah 9:7, the Bible says that there will be no end to the increase of God's government. It doesn't say things will get worse and worse!

The very last words of that verse tell us that "the zeal of the Lord of hosts will accomplish this." The problem is that when the Church needs to be showing forth the zeal of the Lord, we are too often showing apathy and lethargy instead. "If things are only going to get worse and worse anyway, what's the use of trying?" seems to be the attitude.

Now lest anyone misunderstand, let me say very clearly that I am convinced that the Kingdom of God will be *fully* established only when Jesus returns to this planet. I am not saying that Christians can bring the Kingdom in, but I believe that God has called us to play a role in the establishment of that Kingdom.

Jesus told us that we are to "occupy" until He comes. And *to occupy* means "to take or hold possession of." When soldiers are told to occupy a certain territory, they know that they are expected to move ahead and take over territory that is not already under their control. And so when Jesus says to occupy He is telling every Christian to get involved, to be active, to strive to bring everything in this planet under His Lordship.

We have a destiny and a purpose that began before we were even born. Consider Jeremiah 1:5, which says, "Before I formed you in the womb I knew you, and before you were born I consecrated you; And I have appointed you a prophet to the nations" (NAS).

I want everyone who is reading this book to understand one thing: namely, while you were still in your mother's womb, God knew you.

Not only did He know you, but He consecrated you and called you to be a prophet to the nations. Wherever you live, you are called to be a prophet to your nation, your city, and your neighborhood.

Jeremiah was just a sixteen-year-old boy when the Lord called him and he said, "Lord, I don't know how to speak or what to say. I'm just a youth."

But God said to Jeremiah exactly what He says to you: "Don't say you're too young or too old. Don't say you can't articulate well. Don't say you can't get involved, because you will go wherever I send you and speak whatever I tell you to speak."

At first Jeremiah resisted God's call on his life because he was afraid. And that's what's holding many Christians back today—fear.

But again, God's word to Jeremiah, recorded in Jeremiah 1:8, is a guarantee to every believer: " 'Do not be afraid of them, for I am with you to deliver you,' declares the Lord" (NAS).

And 2 Timothy 1:7 tells us that "God has not given us a

spirit of timidity, but of power and love and discipline" (NAS). And in Psalm 34 we are promised that those who seek the Lord shall be delivered from all their fears. Right now, even as I write this book, in the name of Jesus I rebuke the spirit of fear, the spirit of doubt and unbelief in your life, and I release you from any apathy or any lethargic spirit in the name of Jesus. I set you free in the name of Jesus, to be the man or woman of God that He has called you to be.

In Jeremiah 1:9 the prophet goes on to say that "the Lord stretched out His hand and touched my mouth."

If you will allow the Lord to touch your mouth, to speak through you, you will be amazed at what happens. Whenever I get up to speak, I first take a step backward and say, "Lord, take over," and it's beautiful to see what He does. When I give an altar call I don't try to use flowery speech or appeal to people's emotions. Instead, I invite those who want to give their lives to Christ to come down the aisle. Then I turn around, lift my hands to God, and say, "Okay, Lord, it's all up to You."

What am I saying? That unless God touches my mouth and speaks through me, no one at all will respond when I give those altar calls.

I don't want to try to manipulate people or use my personality in any way to influence people. But if God is using you and me to do His will, there is nothing in the world we can't do.

And don't ever say that one person can't make a difference.

I remember how one woman in California, an elderly, gentle little lady who decided to take a stand, changed things in the city of Long Beach. It seems there was a professor at Long Beach State University who was advocating that his students become involved in extramarital and homosexual relationships as "experiments" for a class he was teaching. When this fine Christian woman heard what was going on, she wanted to do something about it. For months, she tried to get the situation changed, but no one would listen to her.

Instead of giving up, she took the story to the media. When they investigated and discovered her allegations were true, they gave the story national coverage. The course was canceled, and no more students were pulled into sinful, deviant sexual relationships under the guise of "academics." Before that one Christian woman became involved, that course had been taught for six years, and dozens of young people had undoubtedly been corrupted by it.

At the University of Hawaii several years ago, the student government had been taken over by a rather hedonistic group. They supported the showing of X-rated movies on campus and used student funds for a number of ungodly things.

Dozens of Christians on campus, mostly those involved with Maranatha, got together and decided to pray and fast to see what the Lord wanted them to do about the situation. They finally decided He was calling them to run against the members of the current student government in the next election. They did, and Christian young people were elected to about ten different offices, including president, secretary, and treasurer.

All three TV stations in Honolulu covered the election of the Christian students. News teams even came to Maranatha church meetings to cover our worship services. And when the students involved in the previous student government demanded a recall vote, the press followed the story.

During this controversy, a forum was held featuring the new student government president and the student who was spearheading the drive to have him recalled. As the cameras rolled, the new president asked the recall leader why he wanted to have him deposed.

His answer?

"Well, ah . . . I . . . ah . . ." And then the recall leader hung his head and said no more.

This picture of defeat spoke eloquently. It was a powerful moment of vindication for the Christians on campus and for Maranatha.

These are two amazing stories, but we all need to be involved in the fight, because there's a war going on out there. And if you want to play it comfortably, you're going to lose.

I have often thought about the fact that when Jesus died on

the cross the Bible records the presence of only one of His apostles. Only John was there, admitting that he was a friend and follower of Jesus. And yet the Bible shows us that John was the only one of the apostles who died a natural death. All the others—those who were afraid to risk their lives—were martyred, according to church historians.

I believe that it was a great honor for the apostles to be able, later, to give their lives for their Lord. But I do find it interesting that only John among the apostles was brave enough to risk death on the day Jesus was crucified, and he outlived the other ten. (And, of course, several of the women who followed Jesus were brave enough to be there with Him at the last, even while the macho apostles ran away.)

Jesus said that if you try to save your life, you will lose it, but if you lose it for His sake, you will find it (Matthew 10:39).

You must be willing to put your life, your reputation, and all of your possessions on the line to join the fight against evil. You cannot just sit idly by and watch the evil continue. Otherwise it will grow to the point where it will be on your doorstep, and you will be totally consumed by the enemy.

In the very first chapter of the Bible, Genesis 1:26, God gives us our marching orders. He says: "Let Us make man in Our image, according to Our likeness; and let them rule over the fish of the sea and over the birds of the sky and over the cattle and over all the earth, and over every creeping thing that creeps on the earth" (NAS).

So, before it had even been formed out of the dust of the ground, God knew that mankind was going to have dominion, to exercise authority over all the rest of the creation. God has never rescinded those orders. The only difference today is that those who have turned against God no longer carry His blessing. But those who are His children, through their acceptance of His Son Jesus Christ, are still called to exercise dominion over all creation.

When He gave the Great Commission, Jesus told His followers to make disciples of all nations (Matthew 28:19). How can we do that? By preaching the Gospel to people and seeing them saved, of course. But if we will understand our job properly, there is much more to it than that. We are called to bring the nation itself to Christ. And the nation is made up not only of the people who live there, but of the arts, the sciences, education, law, political systems, the media, business, and so on—in short, every area of life. And if we are to bring the nations to Jesus, our task is to bring every one of those areas of life under His influence and under biblical principles.

There are four things we need to remember in order to be able to do this:

One, in 2 Timothy 1:9, we discover not only that God has saved us, but that He has "called us with a holy calling." Every Christian has a holy calling on his or her life.

Two, we should be serious about fulfilling our calling. If we treat the Holy Spirit with reverence, why don't we treat our holy calling with reverence? Why do so many Christians think we can just sit around and do nothing until Jesus comes back? Or why do we think we can sit in our easy chairs night after night turned in to the latest offerings on TV and ignore God's calling on our lives?

God has given you special abilities and talents—gifts—and you should be using them. If you don't know what your special gift is (or gifts are), ask God to reveal it to you and work to develop it. Whether God has given you the gift of hospitality, the gift of helps, or the gift of being able to give liberally, whatever it is, you possess at least one very special gift that God expects you to use to fulfill the calling He has put on your life.

Three, God's grace begins where your ability ends. The things you do for God do not depend upon your social status, educational ability, or willpower. God has a purpose and He releases that purpose through His grace. You have to come to the end of your own ability and let God's grace take over.

Four, the Bible says your holy call was granted to you in Jesus from all eternity. In other words, before time even began God had called you. Whenever I think about that, it fills me with awe and gratitude. Even before the moon and stars were created, God called you and me. Before Adam and Eve took their first breaths God knew what purpose He would accomplish through you and me. Even then, He knew every hair on your head, whom you would marry, who your children would be, and on and on it goes. He has a destiny, a purpose for you. Ephesians 1:3–4 reads: "Blessed be the God and Father of our Lord Jesus Christ, who has blessed us with every spiritual blessing in the heavenly places in Christ, just as He chose us in Him before the foundation of the world, that we should be holy and without blame before Him" (NAS).

Verse five goes on to say that He "predestined us to adoption as sons through Jesus Christ to Himself, according to the kind intention of His will."

Some people seem to think they are nothing but accidents waiting to happen, but that's very far from the truth. Whenever you're tempted to berate yourself, to think you're insignificant and couldn't accomplish anything worthwhile if you tried, remember this: God has a plan to bring about His purpose on this planet, and you are an important part of that plan.

Before we go on, I want to say a few words about the call of God in relationship to Romans 8:28. Just about every Christian knows that verse by heart. We hear it said constantly that "all things work together for good," if you love God. But that's not really what the verse says. That's only half the passage. Actually, it says that "God causes all things to work together for good to those who love God, to those who are called according to His purpose" (NAS).

Many people will tell you they love God, but they're not trying to obey His call on their lives. They're not even interested in knowing, many times, what their special calling might be. And because they are not obeying His call, everything is not working together for their good.

Read verse 30: "Whom He predestined, these He also called; and whom He called, these He also justified; and whom He justified, these He also glorified" (NAS).

So, then, we can see that God has a purpose for us as

individuals and He also has a purpose for us collectively, as His sons and daughters.

Christians everywhere need to develop an aggressive mentality. We shouldn't be running from the enemy! Instead, we ought to be chasing the enemy—storming the very gates of hell!

Psalm 115:16 says, "The heavens are the heavens of the Lord; But the earth He has given to the sons of men."

God has given this earth into our keeping, and it is our responsibility to rule it properly. If we Christians don't rule, who will? Atheists and humanists and agnostics, that's who.

Part of the problem, so far as I can see, is that many Christians are fooled into believing there is a benign neutrality that will take over if we abdicate our responsibility. "If we don't rule, somebody else will. He may not be a Christian, but he'll probably be a nice guy, so things will work out okay."

We must realize there is no such thing as neutrality when it comes to God. You are either for Him or against Him, for His Law or against His Law.

If I don't rule in my home, who will? My wife. And if she doesn't rule, who will? The children. And if they don't rule someone else will—quite possibly the state. Someone is always going to rule, whether we agree with what they stand for or not. We Christians can abdicate our responsibilities all we want, but our children and grandchildren will pay a great price for it. We need to be getting believers into city government, boards of education, county commissions, and every other area of government. If we are content to withdraw into a corner and not get involved we are certainly failing in the task God has set before us.

Consider what's going on in this country with regard to abortion. A million and a half unborn children are being slaughtered every year—more than fifteen million since the Supreme Court legalized abortion on demand in 1973— and some Christians sit around singing "In the Sweet Bye and Bye."

We could all serve God better by spending time out in front

of abortion clinics, talking to the women who are going in, and showing them that God does not want them to abort their unborn children. Thousands of Christians, including many involved with Maranatha, are doing just that, and they're saving babies from being killed every day. There are children growing up in Christian homes today because people have talked their mothers out of killing them. And if all the churches would get involved, imagine what a great, great difference we would make in this country.

It's amazing how ignorant of the Bible some of the women are who consider having abortions. If you stand out there and say, "Look, Jesus loves you and He loves your baby," and show them the Scriptures that say that God knew them while they were still in their mothers' wombs, they are astonished. Many of them have no idea what a serious thing they are doing by having an abortion.

Believe me, we've paid a price for what we've done. We've had rocks thrown at us, had people try to run us down with their cars, and had our people beaten up. But we believe saving the lives of innocent babies is worth taking a few hard knocks. But, meanwhile, so many other Christians insist on looking the other way.

One group from Maranatha traveled to a Western city where they were picketing in front of an abortion clinic. A doctor came out cursing and yelling at them and threatening to have them thrown in jail. That Sunday the Maranatha group visited an evangelical Christian church in the same city. Imagine their surprise when they saw that doctor sitting with the congregation.

As soon as the service was over, they asked to talk with the pastor.

"Do you know that one of the members of your congregation operates an abortion clinic?"

The pastor not only knew, but described the doctor as "an active member of this congregation, in good standing."

When our group pressed the issue, the pastor insisted that it was his church's policy "not to get involved in the personal lives of our members." Could it have been that the abortionist's tithes and gifts to the church were more important than the church's taking an active, aggressive stand against abortion?

Christians must take dominion over abortion, and over other areas, too—such as crime.

In Paducah, there was a woman named Mrs. Evans who was a member of the church. She was working in a store when a female robber came in and said, "Give me your money or I'll blow you away."

Mrs. Evans knew her place in God and she just laughed at her.

The bandit produced a gun and told her she meant business.

"Don't you know who I am?" Mrs. Evans asked. "I'm a child of God, and greater is He that is in me than he that is in the world. Your father the devil was rendered powerless two thousand years ago, and I take authority over you and command you to get out of this store!"

The robber made one last desperate demand for the money, whereupon Mrs. Evans pointed her finger at her and yelled, "In the name of Jesus, get out of this store!"

That was all it took. The would-be bandits—a man drove the get-away car—fled. A couple of hours later they were picked up by the police. But Mrs. Evans wasn't through with them yet. She fixed packages of candy, soap, and Christian literature, which she took to them in jail.

The female robber, Sherry, read the Bible and was saved. Mrs. Evans befriended her, loved her, and shared the Lord with her. When Sherry was released from prison, she went to work for a prison ministry, where she has been instrumental in leading others to Christ. She and Mrs. Evans still write each other.

Mrs. Evans was one person who didn't look at the obstacles in her way. She knew that the robber had a gun, but she also knew that God was bigger than weapons and that He had the situation under control.

She understood her place in God, just as Joshua and Caleb did when Moses sent them out to spy on the land of Canaan.

(See Numbers 13:1–14:38.) Twelve spies were sent into Canaan, and ten came back talking about the giants in the land. "There's no way we can defeat these people in battle," they said. "We're like grasshoppers in their sight." Only Joshua and Caleb knew the strength of God. They were the only ones who urged an immediate invasion of the land—giants notwithstanding.

Now, remember, the spies who talked of giants in the land weren't telling lies. There *were* giants in the land. The problem for them was that they were not looking through the eyes of faith. They saw only the obstacles that stood in their way and not God's ability and willingness to help them overcome. In essence, they were saying that those giants in the land were larger than God Himself. Because of that, God said He was grieved with them.

The difference between people of doubt and people of faith is simply that people of faith know that God is bigger than anything that might be in their way. A person of faith takes time to read the Bible; he listens to God, and then does whatever God asks him to do. That's why you'll find such people making a major impact on our world.

I remember a time in Padacuh when a group interested in Eastern meditation held a public meeting in the local library. They wanted to sign up people for their style of meditation, which was clearly a form of worshiping Hindu gods.

James Thomas and a few other believers from our fellowship attended the meeting to see what was going on. They went in and listened to the main speaker talk about the benefits of such meditation and how it was a nonreligious exercise. Then, in the middle of his lecture, he paused and asked for questions.

James had done his homework. He raised his hand.

"Sir," he said, "you've been telling us that this form of meditation isn't a religion, but I have the book right here by the Maharishi himself, and it says on page three-hundred-forty-two that this *is* a Hindu form of religion."

The instructor started to object, but James wasn't finished yet.

"Now why are you saying it isn't a religion, when the man who started it all says right here that it is? Why are you trying to deceive these people?"

Two or three people stood up and said, "We didn't know this was a religion! We're Christians, and we don't want anything to do with this." And they left.

Another woman raised her hand and said, "Well, my doctor told me to come. I have arthritis and I can't move my arm. He thought meditation might help me. Will it?"

"Come here, dear," James said.

When she walked over to him he told her, "You don't have to pay for a course in meditation to heal your arm. God can do a miracle for you right here."

So, then, in front of everyone else, believers and skeptics alike, he laid his hands on her arm and prayed—and she was healed instantly. All the pain left and she began praising and thanking God right in the middle of the meditation meeting.

Naturally, this created quite a stir, and the meditation leader began shouting, "Dismissed! Dismissed! Everyone's dismissed!"

But everyone wanted to talk to James Thomas and the other believers from Maranatha. They prayed for several for healing. Before the evening was over, a young man had surrendered his life to Jesus, and the seed had been planted in several other hearts. And soon after, the library banned the meditation group's meetings!

That's the sort of thing that happens when you have faith and you look for opportunities to make a difference in the world. God will allow you to take even bad things and bring good out of them.

One of the things our people did in Memphis was to wage an all-out war on pornography. They took their cameras and stood in front of one of the city's most notorious pornography shops. Then, when people were about to enter the store, they'd click the shutter and the flash would go off. They didn't even have film in the cameras, but the people whose "pictures" were being taken didn't know that.

After a while, so many customers were being frightened

away that the store owner closed the front entrance. When he did that, a contingent of believers moved to the back door. We stood there with clipboards and made it obvious that we were writing down the license plate numbers of people who were going into the pornography store.

People would come up and say, "Listen, I was really just running over to the grocery store for a minute. Don't write my license number down."

"We won't, if you promise not to come back here."

"Oh, I won't."

In the same city, we also took a stand against the cult groups that were soliciting for donations in the airport, particularly Moonies. They were always there asking for money, and most people didn't know what they were giving to. They'd just throw some money into the pot because they were embarrassed and didn't know what else to do. So we stationed ourselves in the airport, and whenever we'd see one of the Moonies ask for a donation, one of our people would run up and say, "Hey, do you know who these people are? They're Moonies. That's a cult group. You don't want to give money to them!"

"You're right! I *don't* want to give money to them!" And people who had been about to make a donation would change their minds. It was like playing one-on-one basketball. Everywhere they went we were right there with them, making sure they couldn't score any points. After a while, we drove the cult's fund-raisers from the airport.

We had to be willing to risk confrontation and violence, of course. But we wanted to make a difference, and we did.

Another way Christians need to be working to change society is in caring for the poor and disabled. In the early days of this nation there was no reason for a welfare system because the Church took care of the needy. I believe God wants to bring us back to that. The government has had to get involved in caring for these people because the Church has abdicated its responsibility. And I should add that every time the government gets involved in something the Church is supposed to do, it's not done as well. If you want proof of that, just look at the mess our welfare system is in today.

If churches would get back to taking care of their own communities, their own cities and regions, we would have a great revival. We must get back to blessing and helping the poor. Christians should do whatever they can to help, even if it's just going into someone's home and making simple repairs.

There are many other ways Christians can get involved in changing society.

Maranatha Campus Ministries has a rock 'n' roll seminar that we have taken all over the world to expose the demonic aspects of much of today's rock music. Thousands of youth around the world have given their hearts to Jesus as a result of this seminar called, "Rock 'n' Roll: A Search for God." We are currently involved in a major video presentation that will detail exactly what is going on in the world of rock, and explain the demonic symbolism used in the music itself and in the design and packaging of the record albums and logos.

Our Providence Foundation is teaching Christian young people from all over America how to become governmental and political leaders. We have a powerful presentation that explains the Christian origins of this country, and we are in the process of developing a multi-media presentation on the U. S. Constitution. This will be taken all across America to explain how the hand of God was involved in the development of that document. International students are also being trained so they can return and take the lead in government in their own nations.

Many of our people are also helping others by teaching them to read. It is a sad truth that millions of adults in this country cannot read or write. Using a program called "Writing Road to Reading," many believers are working toward change.

One of the most exciting programs in Maranatha Campus Ministries is World Ambassadors. This outreach has the potential to bring millions of people to Christ within the next few years. This, too, is an adventure in which you can play a part. I will talk more about this later.

This is a truly exciting time to be alive. God is moving, and we at Maranatha are thrilled to be a part of what He is doing.

In 1979, at one of our leadership conferences, the Lord said something to me; it was the most astonishing thing I have ever heard Him say. If I hadn't heard it so clearly, I might have been inclined not to believe it.

He said, *Tell the people that more people are going to be saved in the 1980s than all those who have ever been saved in the history of the world. Add up all the revivals of the past and in this one decade more people are going to come to know Me than through all preceding generations put together.*

Yes, God is moving in a mighty, mighty way.

And if you'll allow Him to use you, you will be a big part of it.

One person can make a tremendous difference in this world. It doesn't matter whether he's old or young, black or white, male or female, weak or strong, or anything else. If he is walking close to God, stand back and watch him change the world!

Chapter Ten

Faith Is the Key

The Bible says that faith is "the assurance of things hoped for, the conviction of things not seen" (Hebrews 11:1, NAS).

Faith is also the willingness to risk looking foolish for Christ's sake. There have been many instances when I personally have taken risks in order to obey what I perceived to be a direct word from God, and He has never let me down. It was always a case of "Well, Lord, if I haven't really heard from You on this, I'll wind up looking foolish, but I believe I have heard from You—so here goes." And He has always carried me through.

Of course, even if I had fallen on my face and been the subject of some scornful laughter, what difference would that have made? I would rather err on the side of doing too much than sitting back and doing too little.

If you want to see people won to Christ and the world around you changed for the better, you must have faith. Don't have faith in yourself or faith in your faith, but have faith in God and know that He will be with you and help you in every situation.

If you are a Christian, you should be sharing the Gospel with others. If you're hesitant, you are probably held back because of fear. Many Christians are weak and defeated, afraid of stepping out and declaring their belief in Christ. But if we are going to be about the business of changing this world, we must overcome fear. And faith is the key.

I have already mentioned several areas where we need to get busy. We must, first of all, make sure that we are serious with God, that our lives are totally committed to Him, and that we are walking in holiness and purity by God's grace. We must also learn how to listen to God's voice and be obedient to Him. Then we must understand our authority and responsibility for our nations and change them for the better.

Another thing we must do is learn how to believe. Of course we believe in God. Of course we believe that Jesus Christ died for us. But what I'm talking about now goes deeper. I'm talking about believing in God in your day-to-day affairs. I'm talking about believing in Him enough not to be crushed by every little disappointment that comes your way. And most of all, believing in Him enough to be able to share your convictions with your friends and neighbors, and see many of them won to the Lord.

Some people are held back because they are afraid of what people will think of them or because they don't want to be made fun of. Others are afraid that their friends will reject them. Still others are afraid because they don't know that much. What will they do if someone asks them a tough question and they don't know the answer? Or maybe they're just afraid of people in general. They're shy and don't know how to go about the business of telling anyone about Jesus.

If I'm describing you, then let me tell you again that there is only one antidote to this kind of fear—and that's faith. The Bible says that faith comes by hearing, and hearing by the Word of God. If you want to develop faith, spend more time in the Bible. Soak in it. Meditate on it. Focus on God's promises to His children. Begin to put what you are learning into practice. Then as you see things begin to change in your life, and success in witnessing comes to you, your faith will be increased.

When you pray, ask God to give you the "boldness and

confident access [we have] through faith in Him" (Ephesians 3:12). Repent of your timidity and ask Him to enable you to speak and move with His authority. He will do it.

And, finally, make up your mind that you are going to believe in God and not doubt. Doubt your doubts; don't doubt God! There is a certain component of faith that is an act of the will. If you go on a diet, you make up your mind that you will eat in a certain way and then you do it. In the same way, make up your mind that you are going to believe and then do it! Believe that God will help you win one soul today, and then go out and tell someone about Jesus.

Every Christian should have a planned approach to personal evangelism. It is important to follow the Holy Spirit's guidance, yes, but you need to have a basic structure to follow. Knowing what approach you are going to take will make you feel more at ease, especially at first when you've never done anything like this before. That first time can be tough until you've broken the ice. But when you begin to discover that there really is a spiritual hunger in this world, that people do want to know about God and are willing to listen to you, then telling people about Jesus will be one of your very favorite things. Take my word for it!

I have used The Four Spiritual Laws, as published by Campus Crusade for Christ, another beautiful program called Glad Tidings, and Evangelism Explosion. All three of these are excellent, and I have used each with success. I always take an extra fifteen minutes to make sure the person I am talking to understands the Lordship of Christ, but the point is that many plans for personal evangelism have been used successfully, and every Christian ought to be familiar with at least one of them. Or, if you want to develop an approach that works better for you, go ahead and do it. But in something as important as bringing people into the Kingdom of God, I don't believe in winging it. Many times I've used one of these plans as a basic introduction, and then the Holy Spirit has taken me on from there.

I always pray and ask God for guidance in witnessing. Sometimes He will give me special knowledge about the people I'm talking to and that always gets their attention. Remember, once again, that I am not a unique case. If you learn to hear God's voice, and get your faith level built up, He will do the same for you.

I told you earlier about the young Jewish man who was not interested in hearing about Jesus until God showed me some things about his private life. There have been many other such instances in my life where God has given me "inside information" and has used it to bring people to Christ or to heal someone.

This is what is known as a "word of knowledge," one of the gifts of the Spirit mentioned in 1 Corinthians 12:8. Jesus was using the word of knowledge in John 4:18, when he told the woman at the well that she had had five husbands and was not presently married. She was astonished, because there was no "natural" way for him to have this information.

The same thing occurred in Acts 8:23, when Peter perceived that Simon the Sorcerer was "poisoned by bitterness and bound by iniquity." God is still using this spiritual gift to bring others to Him.

I was preaching in London and a young girl who was paralyzed from the waist down was at the service. She had been brought to the meeting by friends who wanted to know if I would pray for her. She had been prayed for many times, she told me, but believed that one of these times God would hear and would perform a miracle.

But before I began to pray, God revealed to me through the word of knowledge that she was bound up by hatred for her aunt and her mother.

"Young lady," I said, "I believe the Lord has spoken to me and told me that you hate your aunt and your mother."

She didn't try to deny it but, instead, began spitting out her hatred for these two women.

"Yes, I hate them. And I ought to hate them. You don't know what they've done to me!" Her brown eyes were mirrors of her anger.

I held her hand. "That may be true, but are you willing to forgive them?"

She looked back at me without answering.

"I think God wants to heal you, but you're going to have to forgive first."

She looked stunned for a moment. My words had hit deeply. She knew I was right, but forgiving them was not going to be easy. Finally, she said weakly, "Yes, I will forgive. Yes, I do forgive them." A light began to come into her eyes as she was set free from the hatred she had harbored for years. She really had forgiven them!

When I saw that she had truly forgiven, I prayed for her. Then I lifted her up and saw strength go into that body. In a moment she was running around leaping and shouting, grabbing everyone who knew her so she could tell them what God had done in her life. It was a wonderful thing to see.

Another time I was in a movie theater in Paducah watching a showing of "The Cross and the Switchblade" when God spoke to me very clearly. A girl in the theater was on the verge of committing suicide. I was to go to her and say, "God loves you and I love you, too." That was it.

People were not too happy with me when I stood up and began edging my way toward the aisle.

"Hey, down in front!"

"Sit down, will you?"

But I made my way toward her. I couldn't even see her face in the darkened theater.

"Listen," I said, "you don't know me, but I want to tell you that God loves you and I do, too. That's all I'm supposed to say. 'Bye."

Then I turned and walked away. I felt like I was really out there on a limb. The young woman had no idea who I was. She might have thought I was crazy or someone with an unusual way of meeting strangers.

But I knew that was all the Lord wanted me to say at that time, and I also knew that whatever else was on His agenda would be taken care of.

The next night I was preaching in a drug-prevention rally at Tilghman High School. Among those who came forward to receive Christ was a young woman I didn't know—but she knew me.

"You don't recognize me, do you?" she asked.

I hated to admit it, but I honestly didn't know who she was. "No," I said, "I don't. Who are you?"

"I'm the girl you talked to in the theater last night, and I've come tonight to give my heart to Christ."

"Praise God!"

"I just want you to know that I was going to kill myself last night. I had it all planned and even knew exactly how I was going to do it.

"But then, after you came up and told me that God loved me, I decided to wait one more night and see what happened." She went on to tell me that she didn't know for sure why she had come to the drug rally that night, but she had. And when she heard the Gospel, she knew that she was not going to commit suicide. She had found her reason for living and His name is Jesus Christ.

That sort of thing can happen to anyone who learns to live by faith. I can't imagine anything that would be more fun than living this kind of life. You never know what God is going to do next, but you can be sure that it will be something amazing and exciting.

Back when I was still in Long Beach, Christian Life Church had a crisis help-line. One night as I helped answer the phones I received a call, but nobody spoke at the other end.

I was ready to hang up when I felt God urging me to stay on the line. *Don't put the phone down. Sing to the person on the telephone.*

Sing? Well, the only singer in my family is the sewing machine, but if that's what God wanted me to do, I'd do it.

I began singing, very softly, "Praise God, praise God," to the tune of "Amazing Grace."

Sing louder, I heard God say.

Louder? Okay, if that's what You want.

"Praise God! Praise God!"

The other people who were there to answer the phones had

to be wondering what I was doing. Some of them were looking at me as if I were crazy.

Finally, I felt impressed to pray for the "girl" on the other end of the line.

Remember, I still hadn't heard a word, not even a sound, from whoever was on the other end, but I launched out in faith and began to pray for "her."

"Lord, I pray that You would bless this young woman. I don't know what her need is, but You do, and I pray that You would give her peace."

And as I continued to pray, a female voice on the other end of the line began sobbing.

When I said "Amen," she finally spoke.

"You can't believe what I've been through with my parents," she sobbed. "I found your number in the phone book, but after I called I was afraid to say anything."

She went on to tell me that she had been on the verge of slashing her wrists, but decided that before carrying out her plan she would make one last attempt to find some help. When I answered the phone her first instinct was to hang up. But then, when I began singing, she decided for some reason to stay on the line. (And believe me, it wasn't so she could listen to a beautiful voice!)

"And then when you prayed for me, I felt a love and a warmth I've never felt before."

I was able to explain to her that she was feeling the presence of God, and I was able to lead her to Jesus over the phone.

There was another time in Long Beach when a woman called and asked if I could come to the hospital and pray for her son. He was terminally ill with cancer and the doctors had given him three more days at most to live.

He was just twenty-two years old, an athletic, full-of-life young man who was the pride of his mother and father. When I got to the hospital the doctors and nurses tried to talk me out of going in to see him.

"There's nothing you can do," they told me. "It's only a

matter of time. We've prepared his family for it, and if you go in there you'll just get them all upset."

But God was telling me differently, and I insisted on praying for him.

Three days later, instead of dying, the young man was released from the hospital. All of the doctors and nurses at St. Mary's Hospital were absolutely amazed at what had happened, and God received all the glory.

These are the things that happen when you walk in faith and, as far as I'm concerned, faith isn't really faith until you lay it on the line and practice it. Like anything else in life, if you never really use faith it will rust away and become useless.

Some 509 times in the New Testament, God tells us to have faith or believe. When Peter fell, trying to walk on water, Jesus didn't rebuke him for his lack of commitment but because he didn't have enough faith (Matthew 14:28–31). Faith is the key to many miracles.

I was preaching in Sweden when I told the congregation I believed that "God can do anything."

As soon as I had said that, a man stood up—right in the middle of my sermon.

"Do you really believe that?"

"Why . . . yes, of course I do," I answered.

"Well, my wife is in the hospital and she's blind. Can God heal her?"

Inwardly, I was quaking. What had I gotten myself into? But I heard myself say, "Yes, I believe God can heal her."

"Well, then, will you come over and pray for her—right now?"

I assured him that as soon as the service was over a group of us would go to the hospital and pray for this woman. I had faith, and yet my faith was weak. What if God didn't heal her? All of the work I'd been trying to do there would go right down the drain.

Arriving at the hospital, another brother and I prayed together, asking God to give us enough faith to believe Him for this healing miracle. We knew that we were stepping out onto the water just as surely as Peter did when he got out of that boat. We had faith, and yet it was a fearful thing, and we knew our knees were knocking together.

After praying together, we went in and laid hands on her and prayed that her sight would be restored.

"Now can you see anything?" I asked her.

"I can see a little bit of light—a few colors."

We prayed again.

"Now what can you see?"

She was beginning to get excited. "I can see! I can see you!"

My friend and I were mega-excited because God had really come through. We were jumping around and praising God with so much energy that a nurse had to come in and tell us to quiet down. Then, when she saw what had happened, she joined us in our celebration. God honored the faith we had demonstrated by our willingness to pray for this man's wife, and He performed a miracle.

This was truly a major event but, as I've said before, when you learn to be faithful in small things, God will entrust you with bigger things.

This is true when it comes to talking to people about the Lord, too. Exercise your faith. Put your trust in God and see what He'll do. There's a difference between putting God to a foolish test—which is what Satan wanted Jesus to do on the pinnacle of the Temple (Luke 4:9–12)—and trusting Him enough to "go out on a limb" with Him.

And I'll tell you a little something else I've learned over the years. The people who really get angry when you try to tell them about the Lord, who slam doors in your face and tell you to leave them alone, these are the ones who are just about ready to come into the Kingdom. If someone listens to you politely and then says, "Well, that's very interesting. Thanks a lot and I'll think about what you've said," you might have a tough time getting him to commit his life to Christ. But if someone is passionate about it, one way or the other, then watch out. He's like a ripe apple getting ready to fall from the tree!

I learned this lesson about human nature when I was in college and had a part-time job selling music lessons door-to-door. If I could get into someone's living room, I'd set up a little movie projector and show them the company's plan for teaching children to play musical instruments.

I was always excited when I came to a house that had a *No Solicitors* sign posted on the front door. Why? Because I knew I was going to make a sale there.

I'd ring the doorbell and someone would come out with an angry look on his face.

"Didn't you see that sign?"

"Why, yes, sir, I did. But what I have to show you is so exciting that I just knew you'd want to see it anyway."

"Well . . . okay . . . I guess you can come on in."

By that time I didn't need an invitation because I was already in the living room, setting up my projector.

I don't believe I ever missed a sale at a house with one of those signs. You see, I understood why that sign was up there in the first place. As far as I was concerned they might as well have put up a sign saying, "I've had ten other salesmen come by here, and either my wife or I have bought anything and everything they've had to offer. So please, no more salesmen, because we just can't resist."

That's the way it is with people who tell you to stop bothering them about Jesus Christ. What has probably happened is that four or five other people have also told them about the Lord, and they are feeling convicted. Whenever this happens to you, know that the Holy Spirit is dealing with that person or else he wouldn't have responded to you in that way. Instead of being intimidated or frightened, ask God to give you more faith and more boldness. Always remember: the greater the negative response, the greater the possibility that the Holy Spirit is dealing with the person.

A well-known evangelist friend of mine tells a story about taking a wealthy businessman out to lunch because he wanted to talk to him about Jesus. But when he did, the man became so offended that he got up and walked out of the restaurant, right in the middle of the meal. My friend says he was sitting there feeling embarrassed and foolish. He had really blown it, hadn't he? Something about his approach must have been wrong. Now he would never get this man to listen to the Gospel.

But then he remembered what the Bible says. He stood and said out loud, "The Word of God will not return void. I have preached the Word to this man, and the Word will get into his heart, and God will save him."

The next day the man came and sought my friend out. He had been thinking about what he had heard and decided that the evangelist was right. He wanted to give his heart to Jesus.

Remember that the Word of God is sharper than any two-edged sword (Hebrews 4:12) and it will go right into a man's heart. His conscience and his heart will be pricked by the message of Christ—by one Scripture or one thing that you say. Night and day, that Word will haunt him persistently until he comes to know the Lord.

There is much to be said for persistence on your part, too. If you are faithful, you will not give up easily and, as a result, you will see people saved.

The Rev. Paul Yonggi Cho tells a story about a couple who moved into a new neighborhood in Seoul, South Korea. One of the church's home group leaders went to visit them and, just to get them off their backs, the couple agreed to attend a home group meeting. Unfortunately, they didn't like it very much, so they decided not to go back. But every week the home group leader would stop by and invite them to another meeting.

Finally, this couple decided that the only way to get away from this man was to move to another neighborhood, so that's exactly what they did. When the home group leader went by to see them and discovered that they had moved, however, he stopped the postman and got their forwarding address.

Then he called another home group leader in their new neighborhood and gave him their address. As "coincidence" would have it, they had only been settled into their new apartment for a short time when the new home group leader knocked on their door.

"Okay, okay!" they said. "We surrender!"

They knew God was after them, and both the man and his wife knelt down on the floor and, then and there, gave their lives to Jesus.

If you are persistent and keep moving in faith instead of becoming discouraged and retreating, you will see similar things happen. Just remember that Satan is your enemy and he will always try to discourage and intimidate you if you are going about the business of bringing others to Christ. But the closer your relationship to Christ and the more time you spend in private with Him, the stronger your faith will be and the more you will be able to resist the devil and do powerful things for God. Daniel 11:32 says that "the people who know their God will display strength and take action" (NAS).

The bottom line, then, is knowing God. When you know Him, you will be strong and do great things. And there is no way to get to know someone without spending time with him. It's true of people and it's most certainly true of God.

As you spend time with God, especially in prayer and in His Word, the Bible, the more your mind will be transformed. Your mind is something like a computer in that it will only use what information you put into it. You've undoubtedly heard it said before, "Garbage in, garbage out," but it's true. If you spend your time reading trashy novels or watching worthless TV shows, how can you ever expect to build up your faith? But, on the other hand, the more time you spend in God's Word, the more you are scrubbing out doubt, unbelief, and old lustful patterns of life.

When you first receive salvation your spirit is renewed, but your mind isn't. Many Christians don't realize that this is the case. They expect God to snap His fingers and give them a clean and pure mind. If you want your mind to be in tune with the mind of God, if you are going to be a person of faith, you have to soak your mind daily in the Word of God. I couldn't possibly say that too often or put too much emphasis on the importance of spending time focusing on spiritual matters. You should also devote your thoughts to "whatever is true, whatever is honorable, whatever is right, whatever is pure, whatever is lovely, whatever is of good repute," as Paul says in Philippians 4:8, (NAS).

In 2 Corinthians 5:7, the Bible says that we are to walk by faith, not by sight. Verse eight says we are confident if we walk by faith. The King James Version says we are encouraged. Now, since the opposite of being encouraged is being discouraged, I take it to mean we will be discouraged if we turn it around and walk by sight instead of faith.

You see, we can operate in the natural realm or we can supersede that limited realm by moving in faith. For instance, the natural law tells me that if I want to go to Singapore I'll have to get on a boat. Either that or I can try to swim. But there is another law—the law of thrust and lift—that supersedes the natural law of gravity. It doesn't do away with the natural law, but it supersedes it. So now instead of going by boat and taking weeks to get there, I can hop on an airplane and be there in a matter of hours.

If you are feeling discouraged and defeated it's probably because you are walking by sight. You need to understand that faith will cut across all the natural boundaries and obstacles and take you where you need to be!

In 1980 I was doing some speaking at Louisiana State University when I felt compelled to pray against the Mardi Gras and all the drunkenness, lewd behavior, and demonic activity that go along with it. I asked several students to pray with me, telling them that I thought God would close it down if we would join together in prayer.

"They've had a Mardi Gras every year for fifty years," one of the them told me. "I'm sure there'll be one this year."

But I insisted, so we fasted and prayed and believed God. Three days later the banner headline across the front page of the newspaper announced the news: There would not be a Mardi Gras that year. The New Orleans police had gone on strike, and the city would not allow the festival to go on without police surveillance.

The natural law said the Mardi Gras would be held that year, just as it had been for at least fifty years in a row. But the law of faith said it would be canceled, and the law of faith superseded the natural law.

I was talking on the telephone to a fellow pastor in England about his work there when I heard the Lord's voice: *I want you to be on the next possible flight to London.*

The natural law said, "What? Are you kidding? You can't pack up and take off for London just like that. Who's going to take care of things here while you're gone?"

But the law of faith told me I had to be on my way. So, while Rose and I packed my suitcase, my secretary was on the phone making reservations for my flight. I went to London, and the Lord allowed me to see hundreds of people saved.

I had the opportunity, while I was there, to speak in a high school.

The teacher introduced me by saying, "We have Mr. Weiner with us today, and he's going to tell us what he believes about God. Now, you see, I'm an atheist, and I don't believe in God. But I want Mr. Weiner to tell us what he believes and why."

Needless to say, that wasn't the sort of introduction I was used to getting, but after I got up and began giving my testimony, the power of God came upon me. I could tell that many of these boys and girls had been touched by the Lord, so I started to give an invitation. But right in the middle of it the professor jumped to his feet and said, "Now, students, you don't have to believe what he said! You don't have to believe what he said!"

I nodded my agreement with him and said, "He's absolutely right. You don't have to listen to me. The only One you really have to listen to is God. And if God's Holy Spirit is speaking to you right now, stand up and say that you want to give your heart to Jesus."

Seventeen students jumped to their feet and said, in effect, "Jesus Christ is my Lord," right there in a London public high school.

When the class was over, the teacher rushed over to me. I was sure that he would be furious, but he wasn't. He smiled and pumped my hand as if he had enjoyed every word I'd had to say.

"Mr. Weiner, would you please come back and speak to my next class? I know the pupils would love it."

I told him that I would be glad to do that, but at the same time I was certainly surprised by his invitation.

Before that next class began, I stepped to the blackboard and began diagraming man's relationship with God through Jesus Christ. As I did, the professor addressed the class.

"Mr. Weiner," he said, "believes that here is God, and here is man. And it is only through Jesus Christ that man can have a proper relationship with God and become a better creature. I don't believe that. I don't believe in God.

"Here's what I believe," he continued. "I think that if you change man's environment for the better you will change him, too. . . ." and on and on.

When he finished, I took my place before the class and heard God speaking to me, telling me to preach on Psalm 14:1. It didn't dawn on me, at the time, what that Scripture was.

I said, "Young people, in the last class I gave my testimony, but God has instructed me to turn to Psalm 14:1 and teach you out of that Scripture."

When I turned to read it, I nearly fainted. How could I insult someone like this in his own classroom? Well, the Lord said read it, so I did:

"The fool has said in his heart, 'There is no God.' "

Then I said, "Young people, you have been following a fool for more than a year, and now it's time to begin following the King of kings." And I began preaching with the most powerful anointing I had ever experienced.

When I was finished another twenty pupils stood up and gave their hearts to the Lord. And would you believe it? The teacher asked me to come back to his next class—even though the Scriptures had just, in essence, called him a fool! That's the sort of thing that will happen to you when you're operating in the realm of faith.

Following my appearance in those classes I had an opportunity to meet the school's principal, who was confined to a wheelchair. I invited him to a meeting I was holding that night. He came and after we prayed for him he was able to get out of the wheelchair and walk around the auditorium. It was an exciting time to say the least.

But if I had been listening to the "natural" law, I would have been at home in the United States, tending to "business as usual."

One final word on faith. You may feel weak and insignificant but these words of Paul, as recorded in Philippians 4:13, are true for you, me, and anyone else who has ever accepted Jesus Christ as Lord and Savior:

"I can do all things through Him who strengthens me."

Chapter Eleven

Lord, Give Me Compassion

I was in a hotel room near the campus of the University of Kentucky. In four hours, I would be going out to preach the Gospel to hundreds of students. I knew that many, if not most of them, were on a direct route to hell. Unless I, or someone else, could get through to them, they were doomed to an eternity of restlessness and separation from God.

As I prayed for those young men and women, I felt the presence of God in the room with me. And suddenly, unashamedly, I began to weep. I cried off and on for three solid hours. They were my tears, but they were God's tears, too. I knew that His heart was broken because so many of these bright young college students had rejected Him. By doing that, they had rejected the only One who could give meaning to their lives. Well, I cried and sobbed right up until it was time for me to head to the student center ballroom, where the worship service was being held.

When I walked into that ballroom my eyes were still red and I felt as if I might begin crying again at any time. Then I saw the strangest looking young man I had ever seen. He had long, scraggly hair, which was matted and dirty and probably hadn't been washed in a year. He was wearing a long white robe. It, too, was streaked with dirt and was torn. He was barefooted, and a quick glance at his feet told me they were in pretty bad shape, covered with callouses and scabs. This boy obviously spent a lot of time walking.

This young man would have drawn immediate attention to himself, even in the heyday of the campus protest and hippie movements.

He also looked as if he might be a troublemaker, someone who would interrupt my sermon and disrupt the service. But whoever he was, I was filled with the compassion of God for him, and as soon as I saw him my heart went out to him.

During the service he sat quietly and listened, and I kept my eyes on him. I wanted him to be saved and set free from the life of bondage he was living. When I gave the altar call, dozens of students came forward to be saved, but he wasn't one of them.

I decided to go up to him and try to talk to him, but that was nearly impossible. He would only give long, drawn-out, one-syllable responses.

"Young man, did you understand what I was saying tonight?"

"Yaaaaaaaaay."

"Are you ready to give your life to Jesus?"

"Naaaaaaaaaaay."

I asked him several other questions, but that was all I could get out of him. His glassy-eyed stare made me wonder if he was really hearing me at all.

I was feeling desperate.

"Listen, son, I know I'm not getting through to you, but please come back tomorrow. I'm going to have another service in the same place."

I have to admit I was surprised, pleasantly so, when I saw him walk into the ballroom the next evening. Whether he had understood the message or not, at least he had come back. And there was something different about him. Whereas the night before he had sort of wandered aimlessly in and out, tonight there seemed to be a purpose in his steps. He was still dirty and ragged, but I could tell that something was happening.

I was thrilled when, at the end of the service, he came to the altar to give his life to Jesus Christ. We prayed with him, we counseled him, and he was eventually set free from demonic oppression.

We discovered that this young man had been a straight-A student and fraternity member at the University of California, Berkeley, when his search for spiritual answers had led him into a cult. The members wore those long white robes and walked all across America barefooted, living off whatever people would give them. He had been involved with this group for so long that his brilliant mind had all but atrophied. He had been, for all practical purposes, a zombie.

But when he found Jesus, he rediscovered his purpose in life. After being baptized, he went back to school and earned his master's degree.

Today Craig Terndrup is a pastor for the Maranatha Christian Church in Boston. He is a brilliant man, a godly pastor, and he is seeing dozens of students from Harvard, MIT, and Boston University saved. He has scores of students from these universities in his church, and he's brought them into the Kingdom through love and compassion. He is also the composer of "Blow a Trumpet in Zion," a remarkable revival song enjoyed by Christians throughout the world.

He remembers where he was when God saved him, and when you remember the pit that you came from, it's easy to have compassion for others.

Compassion, along with obedience and faith, is one of the key ingredients to seeing people saved and your world changed.

You must have compassion—a genuine love—for the lost, and if you don't, you need to do two things: One, pray that God will give you such compassion, and, two, pray that He will help you remember where you were when He saved you. I don't care who you are or how "pure" a life you may have lived. If you ask God to show you the things that were wrong in your life before He took over, He'll show you—and I can guarantee you that it won't be pleasant viewing.

How important is compassion? First Corinthians 13:1–3 (NAS) puts it this way:

> If I speak with the tongues of men and of angels, but do not have love, I have become a noisy gong or a clanging cymbal. And if I have the gift of prophecy, and know all mysteries and all knowledge; and if I have all faith, so as to remove mountains, but do not have love, I am nothing. And if I give all my possessions to feed the poor, and if I deliver my body to be burned, but do not have love, it profits me nothing.

Just think about this. We can have enough faith to win the world and build great monuments in God's honor and do all sorts of glorious things, but it won't count for anything unless we have compassion. Faith works by love. If you are not moving in compassion, your faith will not operate. Faith never stands alone. Faith stands with love and hope.

Just as a battery must have both a positive and a negative charge to produce electricity, you won't have any power in your life until you have faith and compassion working together. When you read the New Testament notice how nearly every time Jesus performed a miracle it was because he was "moved with compassion."

If you want to see miracles in your life, you must begin to move in faith and compassion.

We've talked before about the fact that many Christians are held back by fear. Well, faith helps us overcome fear, and so does compassion. If we are motivated by godly love, we will not be able to resist talking to people about the Lord because we will want desperately to see them saved.

I wish every Christian would memorize the first four verses of Psalm 103. If we would all do that, we would have a reminder of the way we need to think about our fellow human beings:

Bless the Lord, O my soul;
And all that is within me, bless His holy name.
Bless the Lord, O my soul,
And forget none of His benefits;
Who pardons all your iniquities;
Who heals all your diseases;
Who redeems your life from the pit;
Who crowns you with lovingkindness and compassion.

This Psalm reminds us of all the benefits God has given us. He has pardoned our sins and healed our diseases. We have to remember that we didn't earn any of these benefits. Out of His love and compassion, God simply offered them to us to take as we wanted. If we remember that we didn't earn anything through our own goodness or worthiness, we won't expect other people to prove their worthiness either.

This Psalm also says that He has redeemed our lives from destruction. Psalm 40:2 puts it this way: "He brought me up out of the pit of destruction, out of the miry clay; and He set my feet upon a rock making my footsteps firm" (NAS).

Do you remember the pit you were in before you came to Jesus? Can you recall the loneliness, frustration, and emptiness you felt before He set your feet upon the rock? If you forget the pit you will be unable to relate to the world at large because millions of people are still living in that pit. When you forget, you will have a tendency to be hardhearted, judgmental, pharisaical, and self-righteous.

The Bible says that we are able to overcome Satan by the blood of the Lamb, by the word of our testimony, and by not loving our lives even unto death (Revelation 12:11). Now for the first two or three months after they're saved, most Christians love to give their testimonies. They love to tell what was going on in their lives and how Jesus rescued them. But then, gradually, they stop talking about it. They've been in the church for a while now and have gained some respect. They don't want anyone to know what life was like before Jesus came along.

Sometimes it may be embarrassing for you to share your

189

testimony, but remember it is that testimony that will help overcome Satan. When you give your testimony, it is as if you are getting underneath someone who is listening and pushing him up to Jesus. If you act, instead, as if you think you're better than he is and as if you're stooping down to help pull him out of the pit, he will resent it, and he's likely to resent the Gospel, too.

Take another look now at Psalm 103 and you will see that it says the Lord crowns you with "lovingkindness and compassion." I take that to mean that God has given us the ability to be loving and kind—compassionate. Are we using that ability? How do we treat the people we run into every day? The cashier in the grocery store, the people in the elevator at work, the paperboy? How do we treat our spouses and children? When we're driving, do we cut in and out of traffic like maniacs or show compassion and drive with courtesy and respect? I've heard it said that you can tell the state of a man's soul by watching how he handles himself in rush-hour traffic, and that may be true. But the point I want to make is that if we are not treating people with compassion—if we complain and grumble and cut people down—then we must decide right now to change. We Christians should be noted for our compassion.

I believe, too, that the more kind and compassionate we are, the more good gifts we will receive from the hand of God.

My wife had gone into Shands Hospital in Gainesville to give birth to our son, John David. We were in the birthing room and the nurse who was helping us had such love and compassion in her manner that I had to ask her if she was a Christian.

"No, I'm not." She seemed surprised that I would even ask. "I'm an atheist. Why?"

"Well, you are just so kind to everyone. I've never seen a nurse who was so compassionate."

She laughed. "Thank you." Then she explained to me that she and her husband had tried for ten years to have a baby, but they were unable. She also told me that she was the head research nurse at the hospital and that her husband was a doctor specializing in fertility problems. They had undergone extensive tests that had shown they would never be able to have any children of their own.

When I heard that, I was deeply touched. This woman could have let her childlessness embitter her. She could have resented all the women who came into the hospital to have babies. Instead, she had allowed her own particular trial to build compassion for others within her.

Once again I felt the compassion of God, and tears began rolling down my cheeks. That's when I felt God saying, *You tell her that if she will let you pray for her, I'll give her a baby.*

"Ma'am," I said, "God just spoke to me and told me that if you'll let me pray for you, He'll give you a baby."

For the second time in our conversation, she laughed.

"You don't understand," she said. "It is medically impossible for me to have a baby."

I shook my head, "No, ma'am, *you* don't understand. My Father is the King of kings and Lord of lords, the Creator of all life. And the moment I lay my hands upon you, according to what the Holy Spirit told me, you'll be able to have a child."

With a stunned look, she replied, "Please pray!"

So there in that hospital, with tears rushing down my face out of compassion for that woman, I prayed. Two months later she was pregnant. And within the year she had given birth to a baby boy. I believe God granted her the desire of her heart—even though she wasn't a believer at the time.

Shortly after this happened I told the story at the National Leadership Conference in North Carolina. There was a young Christian couple there—Jimmy and Jan Chamblin—who found themselves in the same situation as this young nurse. They wanted a baby but couldn't have one. They had been trying for years.

After the service they came and asked if I would pray with them.

I didn't hear anything further from them until a few months ago. Jimmy called to tell me they were passing through town on their way to Disney World and wanted to stop by my house.

"You prayed for us a couple of years ago," he said, "and we just want to show you the result of that prayer."

When their car pulled up in front of the house, the first one out was a bouncing, full-of-fire two-year-old boy!

Jan told me, "The doctors told us it was absolutely impossible for us to have children. But we heard you give that testimony about the nurse, and we believed that God would do the same thing for us—and He did!"

They gave me a portrait of the three of them—a beautiful young family. And I love that picture because it reminds me of God's love and compassion.

I believe one of the greatest examples of the compassion of Jesus occurred shortly after John the Baptist was beheaded (Matthew 14:1–12). John was Jesus' first cousin, and so the Lord had lost not only a fellow worker in God's Kingdom, but a relative and close friend. His heart must have been breaking.

The Bible tells us that He wanted to get away by Himself so that He could spend some time alone with the Father. But even in first-century Palestine, the grapevine reacted pretty quickly. It didn't take anytime at all for the word to get out that Jesus was in the area. He had wanted to be alone with His thoughts and His aching heart, but instead He found Himself surrounded by multitudes of people who wanted His healing touch.

They didn't care that Jesus was hurting. They only knew He could heal them. Their thoughts were focused on their own problems. And even so, Jesus was moved with compassion and began healing them, even in the midst of a great tragedy. In fact, it was at this time that Jesus fed the multitude of five thousand with five loaves and two fishes.

We will be able to do wonders if we can come even remotely close to operating in the compassion of Jesus Christ. If you want to see revival come to your city, just go out to your closest shopping mall and watch the crowds of people go by. Pray for them. Say, "Lord, according to Psalm 103, verse four, I have been crowned with lovingkindness and compassion. Lord, give me love for these people. Help me to weep for them." If you pray that, and mean it, He will give you such a compassion that you can't help reaching out to them in the name of Jesus.

You will feel as Jesus did when He saw the multitudes and "felt compassion for them, because they were distressed and downcast like sheep without a shepherd" (Matthew 9:36, NAS). You will ache just as He did—and does—for these lost souls who wander past you, filling up their lives with meaningless diversions. Do you see people who have nothing better to do with their time than hang out in a mall? Doesn't your heart go out to them? Don't you want to show them that there is a purpose and a direction in life?

The Bible says in Psalm 126:5–6 that "he who goes to and fro weeping, carrying his bag of seed, Shall indeed come again with a shout of joy, bringing his sheaves with him."

Who goes forth weeping? The man or woman who has compassion. And what is the seed? The seed is the Word of God that you are sharing with others. So if you are moving in compassion and have the Word of God in your heart, you will return rejoicing because you have led many people to know Jesus Christ. You have produced an abundant harvest of souls.

We must begin to feel compassion for people who are being held hostage by Satan and don't even know it. I learned a lesson about this when I was in Sweden, back in the summer of 1972.

Whenever I preached there I would give an altar call, just as I did at home in the United States. But there was a tremendous spiritual blindness over Europe at that time and we were not seeing much in the way of responses. Even our one-to-one witnessing was not effective. Then we started studying about spiritual warfare and we came to realize that there are spiritual strongholds over people.

After that, whenever I was talking to someone about the Lord, I would first try to look him directly in the eye to discern if there was some demonic power holding him back— whether it was unbelief, fear, or anything else. Then I would ask if I could pray for him and ask the Lord to bless him.

The answer, invariably, was, "Sure. Why not?"

Then, as I prayed for his needs to be met, I would say, "And by the way, Lord, I take authority over that spirit of unbelief" or "that spirit of rebellion" or whatever else it might have been. It was amazing to see what happened. The minute he opened his eyes you could see that things had changed. He couldn't even seem to understand anything about the Gospel before we prayed for him, and then he was open and receptive. I taught our whole team to do this, and we began seeing people saved every single day.

The Bible tells us that Satan has blinded the eyes of the unbelieving (2 Corinthians 4:3–4). But God has given us the power and authority to remove this blindness. We ought to be moving out in compassion to set people free from demonic forces.

Now sometimes we lose our compassion because we lose our zeal for the Gospel. As Revelation 2:4 says, we have lost our first love. Jesus put it this way:

> "I know your deeds and your toil and perseverance, and that you cannot endure evil men, and you put to the test those who call themselves apostles, and they are not, and you found them to be false; and you have perseverance and have endured for My name's sake, and have not grown weary. But I have this against you, that you have left your first love"
>
> Revelation 2:2–4 NAS

I don't have any doubt that many people who read this book have done wonderful things. They are toiling and persevering for God. But it may be true, too, that these things are being done out of a sense of duty—because it is what God expects of them. The only motivation that counts, though, is love. Verse five goes on to say, "Remember therefore from where you have fallen, and repent and do the deeds you did at first; or else I am coming to you, and will remove your lampstand out of its place—unless you repent."

What were our "first works"? Do you remember what it was like when you first became a Christian? Remember how you loved to read the Bible? Remember how much you enjoyed praying—talking with God every chance you got? Sometimes you'd probably go without lunch just so you could read the Bible and pray.

And whom did you talk to about the Lord? Probably just about everyone you came in contact with. Sometimes, some of us didn't use a lot of wisdom or tact, but that's because we were so excited and couldn't wait to tell people what the Lord had done for us.

These are the deeds we did at first. We loved God and maintained our intimacy with Him, and we loved our fellow-man and wanted him to know the compassionate love of God. Today, many of us have grown hard, cold, compassionless, and we don't even realize it. Some of us are too busy to see that the flame is flickering and in immediate danger of going out forever!

Before you respond too quickly that this has not happened to you, please examine your life and make sure. It can happen to anyone. There's plenty of evidence in the New Testament that it happened to many of Jesus' followers, including the twelve apostles.

Consider this: A blind man sits by the roadside calling out for Jesus to heal him. And what do those who are with Jesus do? They tell him to shut up, to leave the Lord alone (Luke 18:35–43). I'm afraid that those people would be right at home in some of our churches today. I can just hear one of them on the telephone:

"You want to make an appointment with Jesus? Well, let me check His calendar. I'll tell you what: He takes appointments on Tuesdays and Thursdays, but don't call after 4:30 P.M. or on weekends. . . ." I don't think that's the way Jesus would do it.

I believe any Christian has to use wisdom in these things. We have to set parameters that allow us to spend time with our families, and everyone has to have some time alone. But I also believe we have gotten 'way out of balance and need to rediscover the compassionate ministry that God has called each one of us to.

I mentioned about the feeding of the five thousand and how this was an amazing demonstration of the compassion of Christ. I believe it is also a pretty amazing example of the apostles' lack of compassion.

Here was Jesus preaching to five thousand people, and the disciples came running to Him:

"Hey, Lord, come on. Let's go. It's past twelve noon, so the worship hour is over. Send these folks on home so they can buy their own food to eat. We're tired. We've worked hard today, so why don't you get these people out of here?"

I'm sure that the Lord must have looked at those disciples with tears in his eyes, wondering if they would ever learn. And then, moved with compassion, He took those five loaves and two fishes, and looked up to heaven and thanked His Father for them. I have always found it interesting that Jesus looked up to heaven when He gave thanks. He didn't look at the problem—at the tiny amount of food he had, or at the huge multitude waiting to be fed—but looked instead, toward heaven, and the solution.

Then He took those loaves and fishes and began passing them out. The first person took some, but there were still five loaves and two fishes in the basket. The second person took some, then the third, and the fourth. And—what was going on here? Now it looked as if there were at least five fishes and nine loaves in the basket! And on it went, until everyone had eaten all they wanted. And you know what? There were leftovers! There will always be leftovers—more than enough—when compassion is in operation.

But what about the apostles? I believe their hearts had become hardened. They had lost their first love and their sense of why they were on this earth in the first place.

If you are a Christian, your purpose is to see people saved, to be an ambassador for Jesus Christ. You may be a doctor, but you're an ambassador for Christ first and a doctor second. Or you may be a teacher, but you're an ambassador for Christ first and a teacher second. Whatever you may be—lawyer, house-wife, engineer—your service to Jesus must come first.

I knew a man who wondered out loud why his children

were so worldly, especially when he tried so hard to serve the Lord. But as I looked at his life I could see clearly why his children acted as they did. God didn't come first in that man's life. No way! He was going along with the world and trying to make his Christianity fit into the "modern scene." He wasn't fooling anyone with his halfhearted lipservice to Christianity—least of all his children.

But if your children see that God comes first in your life—that you are moving with compassion and are interested in winning souls—then they'll fall into step right alongside you. They won't be worrying about the latest fads or whether they've experimented with this or that drug. Instead, they'll be operating in compassion, winning souls, and changing the world for Jesus.

Before you go on to the next chapter, I encourage you to examine your own life to see if you are really moving in a spirit of compassion. If you're not, just renounce any religiosity or any hardness of heart. Repent of it and return to your first love. Remember the pit that you were in before Jesus found you. Try to remember what it was like down inside that pit: the loneliness, the discouragement, the God-shaped vacuum in your heart that could never be filled except through knowing Him.

Remember how you looked here and there for answers but couldn't find anything but frustration and disillusionment until Jesus came along and rescued you. Remember that there are at least 2.5 billion people in this world who haven't had even one chance to hear the good news of Jesus.

And then, once your heart has melted with compassion, move out with weeping to set the world free.

Chapter Twelve

Reaching the World From Your Doorstep

Mengistu Haile Mariam was serving in the armed forces of Ethiopia. He was a bright young man and demonstrated leadership qualities that marked him for an excellent future. Largely because of those qualities he was sent to the United States for further military training at Fort Leavenworth, Kansas.

He was delighted to be in America—but not for long. He soon discovered that there were many places he could not go simply because of the color of his skin. He was denied service in restaurants. He was ordered to sit at the back of the bus. He was sometimes taunted and made the butt of practical jokes—all because he was black.

By the time Mariam was ready to go back home to Ethiopia, he hated this country and everything it stands for. Because he was so disillusioned with the United States, his allegiance shifted toward the Soviet Union. He waited and plotted and looked for the opportunity to make his move. It finally came.

Today Mengistu Haile Mariam is the Communist dictator of Ethiopia. His repressive policies have undoubtedly worsened conditions in that country, and some say they have contributed to the famine that has killed thousands of people there during the 1980s. He has persecuted the Church, thrown his political opponents into prison, and led his country into an orbit around the Soviet Union.

And he has never forgotten that in the United States some people called him "nigger." Now that may not be the only reason Mariam chose the path he did, but it most certainly contributed.

Or consider what happened to Yosuke Matsuoka and Isoruku Yamamoto of Japan. Matsuoka came to this country to attend the University of Oregon, and Yamamoto, Harvard. Once again, both men encountered racial prejudice and left this country embittered. A few years later, Matsuoka was serving as Japan's foreign minister, and Yamamoto was the commander of the combined fleet. Matsuoka helped conceive the plan for Japan's surprise attack on Pearl Harbor that propelled us into World War II, and Yamamoto actually led the attack!

These are only three of the men who have come from other countries to study in the United States and have turned against this nation while they were here. There are, sadly, many others.

Think how different history could have been if these men had met with a different reception here. What if an American family had befriended Mariam, had taken him into their home for dinners and invited him to picnics and other outings with them?

What if Matsuoka and Yamamoto had found love and compassion here instead of prejudice and ridicule?

And, finally, what if some compassionate Christian had shared the Gospel with them?

It's too late now, of course, to change what has already been done, but the important question is: "What about tomorrow?" There are hundreds, even thousands, of Mengistu Haile Mariams in this country right now. And this time, we had better make the most of our opportunity to reach them.

That's what Maranatha's World Ambassadors program is all about, and as far as I'm concerned it is one of the most exciting things we have ever done. Jesus commanded His followers to take the Gospel into all the world (Mark 16:15, Matthew 28:19). We can do that simply by reaching the international students that are already studying on American college campuses.

In Maranatha we have already seen nearly three hundred students from somewhere around fifty nations accept the Gospel through World Ambassadors. We are teaching and discipling them, so that when they go back to their native lands they will be able to tell their fellow countrymen about the Lord.

We have already seen new churches planted in eighteen countries on five continents, and that number is growing so fast that by the time this book goes to the printer it will undoubtedly be outdated.

The world is at our doorstep, and every Christian church in America should be making some sort of effort to reach out to these international students. It is rare for any college not to have at least a few foreign students, and most of these are the cream of the crop. They are almost always within the top five percent of their nations' scholars. They are sons and daughters of presidents, kings, and queens. They, themselves, are the future presidents, kings, and queens. They will be doctors, lawyers, teachers, and will assume other respected positions within their societies.

If you reach these men and women you are reaching the future leaders of nations, and you are making an impact that will be felt around the world for many years to come.

In 1987 there were 344,000 international students representing 188 nations studying in the United States. And, according to our figures, 67 of those 188 nations restrict traditional Western missionary activity. In other words, these nations are closed to the Gospel.

Many countries have held hostility toward American and European missionaries whom they viewed as foreigners coming in to impose a "foreign religion" on the people. It's true, too, that there are cultural barriers between foreign missionaries and native people. But the people in Malawi will listen to one of their own. So will the people in China or India or any other country, all around the world.

The United States is a melting pot, just as Jerusalem was on the day of Pentecost. Have you ever wondered why God chose the day of Pentecost in the city of Jerusalem to give the apostles the gift of the Holy Spirit?

Read Acts 2:8–11:

"And how is it that we hear them in our own language to which we were born? Parthians and Medes and Elamites, and residents of Mesopotamia, Judea and Cappadocia, Pontus and Asia, Phrygia and Pamphylia, Egypt and the districts of Libya around Cyrene, and visitors from Rome, both Jews and proselytes, Cretans and Arabs—we hear them in our own tongues speaking of the mighty deeds of God."

Jews from all around the world had come to Jerusalem for the Feast of Pentecost, and God used that opportunity to reach them with the Gospel. From there, they went home, and the Church began to grow throughout the entire world.

We have the same conditions here in America today, and we must learn to take advantage of the situation.

In fact, I would go so far as to say that the Bible *commands* us to teach these foreign students about the Lord. There are several passages that touch on the topic. Remember that the words *stranger* and *alien* have been translated from the original Greek or Hebrew words meaning "one of foreign birth."

Assemble the people, the men and the women and children and the alien who is in your town, in order that they may hear and learn and fear the Lord your God, and be careful to observe all the words of this law.   Deuteronomy 31:12, NAS

He executes justice for the orphan and the widow, and shows His love for the alien by giving him food and clothing. So show your love for the alien. . . ."   Deuteronomy 10:18–19, NAS

When a stranger resides with you in your land, you shall not do him wrong. The stranger who resides with you shall be to you as the native among you, and you shall love him as yourself. . . .   Leviticus 19:33–34, NAS

Then the King will say to those on His right, 'Come, you who are blessed of My Father, inherit the kingdom prepared for you from the foundation of the world. For I was hungry, and you gave Me something to eat; I was thirsty, and you gave Me drink; I was a stranger, and you invited Me in. . . .   Matthew 25:34–35, NAS

That last verse is, to me, one of the most powerful. When Jesus spoke of the coming judgment He equated Himself with a foreigner and said that whatever we do to the foreigner among us is what we are doing to Him.

Pretty frightening words for those who hurled insults at Mengistu Haile Mariam, Yosuke Matsuoka, and Isoruku Yamamoto.

If you want to know how important it is to reach internationals with the Gospel message, take a look at the eighth chapter of Acts. Philip was preaching revival after revival and seeing scores of people saved. All of a sudden an angel spoke to him and told him to go down into the desert because there was one man traveling along that road whom Philip was supposed to preach to.

That may not make sense to us. Why should Philip stop his successful crusade to go down and stand along the road that ran from Jerusalem to Gaza, just so he could preach to one man? Who was this man, and why was he so important? He was an Ethiopian, "a eunuch of great authority under Candace the queen of Ethiopians." He had been in Jerusalem and was on his way back home.

You know the rest of the story. Philip found the man, preached the Gospel to him, and baptized him. The Bible also tells us that the eunuch "went on his way rejoicing." What the Bible doesn't say, but what undoubtedly happened, was that when the eunuch got back to Ethiopia he talked about Jesus to anyone who would listen, and, as a result, the Church was established in that country!

If God thought it was important for Philip to reach out to an international with the Gospel, why don't we in America learn from this example?

The Communist countries understand the importance of reaching out to internationals. The Soviet Union in particular has taken the lead in offering college scholarships to students from Third World countries. For instance, in 1985 Communist nations offered more than 14,000 fully paid scholarships to students from Latin American and Carribean countries. By contrast, the United States offered around 1,200. The Soviet Union handed out 1,653 scholarships to students from Costa Rica alone, while the generous United States offered 43. Costa Rica has long been known as a bastion of democracy and stability in Central America. How long do you suppose that will remain true when her top students are being educated in the Soviet Union?

It shouldn't be the Communists who are rushing to befriend these young men and women! It ought to be the followers of Jesus Christ. It's amazing, isn't it, to see the zeal with which the followers of a godless, antihuman philosophy such as Communism pursue their goals, while many Christians sit back and do as little as they possibly can and still sneak into heaven?

Why do the Communists have this emphasis? Because they know current statistics show that fully fifty percent of all the world leaders of the next twenty-five years will be trained at universities in the United States. They know that some forty prime ministers and presidents who are currently in office studied in Western universities. (Jose Napoleon Duarte of El Salvador studied at Notre Dame, Corazon Aquino of the Philippines at the College of Mount St. Vincent in New York, and on it goes.) They hope to reach these people with their godless philosophy before we reach them with Christ. We can't let them succeed.

At Maranatha we're originating programs to reach out to

these students. We're helping them with their English, using the Bible as a textbook. We set up tours to take them to amusement parks and museums, and we invite them into our homes. We want them to learn about our culture and our history, and we are forming lasting friendships.

I have seen surveys in which foreign students are asked what they hope to gain from their time in the United States. Invariably the students say the thing they want most is an American friend. And as Mark D. Rentz, writing in *Newsweek* magazine ("My Turn," February 16, 1987) says, "Making a foreign friend is one of the easiest things in the world to do. They don't necessarily need us to do things for them, they just need us to do things with them. They are, by and large, courteous, ambitious, bright and sociable."

Rentz goes on to point out that the United States government spends $15 billion every year in foreign aid. He talks about the fact that we have sent more than 100,000 people overseas through the Peace Corps since 1961. But he also points out that "when we entertain strangers in our midst, instead of saying, 'Welcome to our home,' the words many foreigners seem to hear, expressly or not, are 'Go home.' " It is truly ironic that we "alienate on our own soil the citizens of nations we journey great lengths to influence."

The last words of his column are: "The next wave of world leaders is here. Influence the world; go and make a foreign friend."

To this, I can only add "Amen" and that we will make an even greater impact on the world if we bring that foreign friend to Christ.

It is to this end that we have just started an organization called "American Friends of Foreign Students," and the foreign students are loving it because it gives them exactly what they want—an American friend. We have organized activities on campuses throughout the United States.

In some places, such as at the University of Minnesota, we work with the student government. At Minnesota we also have dinners every week—sort of "get acquainted" affairs, where international students and Americans meet for an evening of sharing and getting to know each other. We encourage our people to invite these students into their homes, to, in effect, take it upon themselves to adopt one of them. And, believe me, not all of the benefits go to the internationals. I have had many Americans tell me how much this program has enriched their lives as they have developed lasting friendships and had their eyes opened to the beauty and knowledge of other cultures.

Once, when I was speaking at The Church on the Rock in Rockwall, Texas, I gave an altar call for those who would commit themselves to reaching out to foreign students. Specifically, we would start off by inviting those students into our homes for Thanksgiving dinner. More than 300 people came forward. I told them that some of us would be going out to visit area campuses, and we would be inviting students to dinner. More than 300 contacts were made. Now, admittedly, not all of these students will accept the Lord, but I have no doubt that some of them will.

Think of what would happen if we could get 1,500 churches to join the World Ambassadors program—not an unreasonable figure. If each of those churches were able to win ten people to Christ in a year, at the end of that time we would have an army of 15,000 missionaries. In three years we would have 45,000 missionaries—more than the total number of Protestant missionaries from the United States serving throughout the world right now. And what is even more exciting to me is the fact that these students would be even more effective than missionaries currently in the field.

Don't misunderstand me because I am in no way criticizing our trained missionaries. The men and women who have entered missionary service deserve nothing but praise and credit. But as I said before, people are more likely to listen to someone who is a member of their culture—especially someone who is in a leadership position within that culture. And, also, there are many countries where foreign missionaries are not allowed, period.

So far I've been talking about what could happen here in

America, but I need to point out that this plan will and has worked in other countries, too, such as Australia.

There are 12,000 international students there. A few years ago one of them was a young man from Thailand. During his time at Melbourne, a Christian man reached out to him and eventually won him to the Lord. He stayed in Australia for five years where, in addition to his studies at the university, he was trained for leadership in the Christian church.

Then he went back to his native country and started a church there. Today that church, with 1,500 members, is the biggest in Thailand. But that's not all. He's started four other churches, too, and has been, in fact, the most successful missionary Thailand has ever seen!

Another young man returned to Indonesia from an American university determined to gain a foothold for Christ in that predominantly Moslem nation. He invited a speaker and rented a soccer stadium for three nights in a row. He had no idea how many people would show up to hear the Gospel, and some scoffers said the preacher would probably be talking to an empty stadium for three nights. Instead, there wasn't an empty seat in the place and some 30,000 people came forward to pledge allegiance to Christ. And all because Christians in America reached out to one young man.

A church in Guatemala was started by a student, Roberto Quezada, who had been discouraged and lonely. He was traveling from Guatemala to Mississippi State University when he decided he couldn't take it anymore. Upon arriving at the airport in Starkville, Mississippi, he had actually decided to return home when an American asked him where he was going. The two of them struck up a conversation, and Quezada was soon convinced, by his new American friend, to give it another try. The friend was a Christian and he led Quezada to the Lord.

This young man had contacts in high government places, and when I flew to Guatemala for an audience with then-President Rios Mont, he went with me.

I hope that what I'm telling you is making you excited about what you can do. I hope, further, that you'll be so excited you'll move ahead and do something! Reach out the hand of friendship to a foreign student in your city. Or perhaps you will want to become a member of our World Ambassador program. You can do that by calling (904) 375–6000, or by writing World Ambassadors, Post Office Box 1799, Gainesville, FL 32602.

But before you do anything—a word of caution. You must really want to be a friend to these students. If you think you will win one of them to Christ and then move on to the next one, you're not approaching it correctly. The most important thing is to be a friend, pure and simple. These youngsters are extremely bright and perceptive, and if they can see that you are feigning friendship simply because you want to convert them to Christianity, they won't buy it. Furthermore, they won't buy you, and they won't buy your religion.

I know of an Indonesian student at the University of Tampa who was befriended by a Christian family that lived in the suburb of Brandon, more than a half-hour's drive away. These people really reached out to the young man. They had him in their home at least one night a week for a year. This meant driving into Tampa to pick him up, driving him home for dinner and then, once the evening was over, taking him back to school.

For most of that time the young man showed no interest at all in religion in general or Christianity in particular. But the family didn't press. They invited him to go on picnics with them; they included him whenever they could in family outings. They never hid their Christianity from him and they would invite him to church with them. But when they started to talk to him about the Lord he would back off, and they'd let the matter drop. But all the while, the witness of this Christian family was before the young man's eyes.

Imagine how wonderful these people felt when the young man told them the life they were living had convinced him. He wanted to make Jesus Lord of his life, too! It might never have happened if he hadn't seen that the members of this family genuinely loved and cared for him.

Even if a student doesn't give his heart to the Lord, he still can be an important contact in a country. I know of another student from Taiwan who, despite years of friendship with Christians from Maranatha, never did become a Christian. But as he was preparing to return to his native country he said, "You have been so good to me and I want to help you. If there is ever anything I can do for you in Taiwan, just let me know." We *have* let him know and, true to his word, he has opened many doors for us there. This doesn't mean, of course, that we have "given up" on him. I still expect that he will one day decide to follow Jesus, but in the meantime he is our friend and he knows we really care about him as a human being.

If there is one thing these international students can teach us, above everything else, it is what friendship really means. I have had many of them tell me the same thing: that Americans' concept of friendship is often superficial. Too often, they say, we have "acquaintances" rather than "friends," and I have to admit this is true. A friend, in their estimation, is not someone who has you to dinner once or twice, and with whom you can enjoy a few moments of lighthearted conversation. A friend is someone you can talk to, someone who will listen to your innermost thoughts and fears and share his with you. International students are looking for Americans who are interested in developing that kind of relationship.

We have had dozens of "success" stories; I want to share a few more with you.

The first one that comes to mind is Dr. Tsukasa Ito. Dr. Ito came from Japan to do research at Shands Hospital in Gainesville. My sister, Jerilyn Stillwell, and her family reached out to him and had him in their home on many occasions. In the course of a year's friendship with him, they learned many things about Japanese history and culture. He, in turn, learned much about the life of an average American family. Make that an average American *Christian* family. After a year, Dr. Ito made a decision to give his life to Christ.

Then, when his research was finished, he returned home where he became a leader in the church. Now it is not easy to evangelize in Japan because this proud culture is steeped in the traditions of its own religions—primarily Shintoism and Buddhism. Japanese are often willing to grant Jesus Christ a place among their list of deities, but they are not so often willing to give Him the place He deserves, as the only begotten Son of God. But Dr. Ito has been instrumental in following up and establishing a firm foundation in the lives of new believers.

That's not all that happened through my family's relationship with Dr. Ito. My niece, Julie, who was twelve at the time, became fascinated with Japan through her talks with him. Two years later, when she was fourteen, she went to Japan during the summer as part of a missionary team. She was able to help teach English at a university there, and some of the students she taught accepted Christ. Through Dr. Ito she had not only developed the desire to take the Gospel to Japan, but she also received insight into Japanese thinking that gave her rapport with her students and enabled her to relate to them on a deeper level.

Also, primarily because of Dr. Ito, the other children in the family were influenced to support missions. They came to see that there really are millions of people in the world who have never had a chance to hear the Gospel, and they became determined to do whatever they could to change that situation. Another benefit, then, of reaching out to international students is that your entire family, including your children, can come to understand what missionary work is all about and why it is so important.

Another one of our successes occurred when a student from Malaysia gave her heart to Jesus. She had been attending World Ambassadors dinners for more than six months but had told her best friend, who was also from Malaysia, that she was coming simply for the meal and the conversation.

"Don't worry about me. I'll never become a Christian."

Whenever anyone tried to talk to her about the Lord, her response was the same. "I'll never become a Christian."

When time came for our International Student Conference in Seattle during December of 1986, she decided to go. It was there that she realized the Holy Spirit was speaking to her and she responded to an altar call to give her heart to Jesus.

When she got back home and told what she had done, her friend was shocked.

"I don't understand it," she said. "You told me you would never become a Christian. What happened?"

When she heard what happened, and as she saw the dramatic change in her friend's life, she, too, was convinced and decided to become a Christian.

The second young woman was baptized in church the following Sunday and after her baptism stood in front of the congregation to give her testimony. Another young man from Malaysia, someone we had been trying to reach for some time, heard what she had to say. He then decided that he, too, wanted to accept Jesus Christ as his Lord and Savior. Talk about the domino principle! One of these young people had been a Moslem. All may face some problems when they return to Malaysia because of their allegiance to Christ, but they're not worried about that. They are among the happiest and most joyful people you could ever want to meet. At long last they have a real reason for living, and I predict that they will make a major impact for the Lord in their native land.

Another student from Singapore became a Christian at the University of Minnesota. He was so excited he couldn't wait to share the news with several of his friends who were also in the United States attending college. He called them and asked if they would come to Minneapolis for a visit because he wanted to tell them what had happened in his life. They were so intrigued by this that several of them traveled hundreds of miles to get there. They weren't disappointed by what he had to tell them—and many of them accepted the Lord, too.

He was excited when he found Jesus! Why aren't we that excited about Him? We certainly ought to be. That's another benefit of reaching out to the international students. When you see how excited they become when they enter into a relationship with Jesus, it will remind you how much you have to be excited about as a child of God!

There are eleven reasons why we in Maranatha reach out to international students, and I want to review them with you:

1. Because it is the will of God.

2. Because the visiting international students are sometimes from countries that restrict or are resistant to missionary activity. If we are going to reach these countries with the Gospel, we can do it best by reaching those who come to this country to learn.

3. They are destined to be the leaders of their nations. If we reach them for Jesus, the course of history can be changed.

4. They will not meet with the suspicion and mistrust that usually hampers American and European missionaries.

5. They already know the language and customs of their countries so we will not have to spend years training them for life in a certain region. In this way, they are already "equipped to serve."

6. They are accessible and responsive to friendship.

7. Nothing can have more of an impact for missions on an American church than personal participation by its members in a ministry to international students. As an example of that, consider what happened through my sister's family's relationship with Dr. Ito.

8. By reaching internationals here in America and encouraging them to return to minister to their own societies, we can cope with the financial requirements. As an example, again consider Dr. Ito. He is a doctor by profession who realizes that his first allegiance is to Christ. He is a pillar in the church in Japan where he gives his tithes and offerings.

9. When internationals carry Christianity to their own lands, more Americans are free to witness to nations that have no other access to the Gospel.

10. When international students return to their countries, they usually support other workers. They begin to send out their own missionaries.

11. Those who are converted and discipled here will likely hold leadership positions in churches in other lands. Thus they will gain the respect of non-Christians and attract those otherwise-alienated members of their societies. In other

words, when influential members of society come back home—doctors, lawyers, and so on—saying that they have accepted Christ, they are going to have a tremendous influence on other educated members of society. As an example, consider India. In that country Christianity has made tremendous impact among the lower castes, who are delighted to discover that God loves them and that they are not inferior to other people. But among the higher castes, who have much to lose (or think they do, anyway), the Gospel has met with resistance or indifference. If we can reach members of the higher castes who are in America to study, they will return home and begin churches among the higher caste Hindus.

These eleven reasons were outlined by Dr. Mark Hannah and they explain well why we target international students for conversion.

Hand-in-hand with these, there are seven other reasons why we in Maranatha have targeted the college campuses in particular for evangelistic outreach, and I want to share these with you also.

1. The university campuses are where the future leaders of the world are being educated.

2. The campus is where most of the great revivals in history have started. In 1903, Vladimir Ilich Lenin took seven university students and fashioned them into a movement. The rest is unfortunate history. Nearly every movement, good or bad, begins with the youth, and usually on the university campus. According to historians nearly all of Jesus' apostles were men in their twenties. Peter was probably in his thirties, and Mark, who wrote the Gospel that bears his name, was probably a teenager.

3. The values of the campus will become the values of society within ten years.

4. The campus is where the most available and trainable masses of people are. That's why the Communists spend so much money trying to infiltrate it.

5. The campus is a small city. When we change the campus, we learn how to change the city, state, and nation. When Christian students learn how to assume leadership roles

on the campus, they'll be learning how to govern cities, states, and nations after they have graduated.

6. Education is not neutral. It will cause people either to respect God and His principles, or to turn away from Him.

7. God promised to pour out His Spirit on all mankind and said that the sons and daughters would prophesy (Joel 2:28). These sons and daughters—many of whom are on the college campuses—will be the ones who will preach the Gospel and change society.

These are the specific benefits from reaching students in general and international students in particular.

And it's not that hard to do.

I know of a man in California who throws pizza parties once a week for foreign students—mostly Moslems. He also asks if any of these students would like a "conversation partner," someone who will meet with them for just thirty minutes every week to practice English. Many of the students are not only willing but delighted to take him up on this. Some of the people in his local church have volunteered to serve as conversation partners, and they usually use the Bible in these English lessons.

Maybe you don't have the money to feed a dozen or so international students once a week, but surely you can have one student to dinner. If there's not a college in your community, chances are there's one within thirty minutes of you where international students are enrolled. Call the college's switchboard and ask if there is an organization of foreign students on campus. If that doesn't help, ask for the office of the campus newspaper. The editor ought to have a list of every organization on campus along with the current officers, and if he doesn't, he can probably give you the names of one or two international students.

Once you've taken that first step, it's easy to begin developing those "hands-across-the-water" friendships.

In our World Ambassadors program making friends is not the final step. Neither is bringing these students to Christ. Once we have done that, we begin organizing a church. For example, we had a number of students from Jakarta, Indonesia, accept Christ. We began training these young people in the various aspects of church leadership. One man was a natural speaker, very much at home in front of a crowd, so we trained him to be a pulpit minister. A young woman with a knack for meeting strangers and making them feel at ease was given special training in the field of visitation and evangelization. Another student was trained in leading corporate worship.

By the time these students were ready to return to their native country, they knew each other well, they were able to work together, and each was an expert in a specific area of church leadership and development. What we did, in essence, was to send an entire, contextualized church back to Indonesia.

This is one of the reasons that our church there is experiencing tremendous growth, even in the midst of a hostile situation. We were able to "hit the ground running," so to speak, and have experienced tremendous growth from day one.

One of the first things those students did on their return to Indonesia was to rent a hotel room and begin holding worship services. I flew over and held a meeting. Two hundred people accepted Christ, and one hundred of these said they wanted to be a part of this new church. I told these new believers to study our "Fundamentals of Faith" course and said I would be back in six weeks to see what they had learned and test them. When I returned in six weeks, I discovered that eighty percent of them had stuck with the course and passed the test.

While I was there I preached in a week-long crusade and another two hundred people were saved. I did the same thing—told them to study for the test and said I'd be back in six weeks. This time I handed out one hundred diplomas. There were now two hundred and twenty members, and the congregation had outgrown the hotel meeting hall!

In December 1986 our first International Students Conference, to be held annually, attracted one hundred and fifty students, from thirty-nine countries. In December of 1987 we tripled that number with nearly four hundred and fifty internationals attending. These students gathered together to learn how to be church planters in their countries. It was thrilling to see them become excited about starting churches, and it was also thrilling to see them meeting all of the other new Christians from their homelands and having the joy of such fellowship for the first time.

Another thing we do is keep computer lists of all our foreign students—and we do our very best to keep it updated. Then if we want to know what is going on with regard to, say, Taiwan, all we have to do is put a disk in the computer. The list tells us how many Taiwanese are in our program and when they are going back home. Then, if five or six students are going back to Taiwan at the same time, we get them in touch with each other and organize them into teams. All of this is a tremendously effective way of introducing the Gospel into a foreign culture.

If this all sounds too complicated and sophisticated for a local church, I want to remind you that it doesn't take this sort of organization to have an impact for Christ on a global scale. All it takes is to reach one international student, and anyone who is really serious about evangelism can do that.

The idea of reaching international students with the Gospel is not new. In fact, in 1924 the great Christian leader Robert Speer called American Christians to recognize the opportunity that lay before them. Today, more than fifty years later, the words he spoke are truer than ever and it is urgent that we finally pay attention to the vision of this great man. He said: "American life and the Christian Church have never met a more severe and searching test than they are meeting today in the presence of these foreign students in our schools. These young men and women from many lands are testing the honesty of the political and social axioms which have consti- tuted our American tradition. They are proving the reality of our profession of Christian brotherhood and equality."

He went on to say, "Almost all of them came full of confidence and hope. Many of them are going back disillu- sioned, some bitter, some sorrowful. Some found that the

Christianity they had acquired from American missionaries was not confirmed by the Christianity they met in the land which had sent the missionaries forth.

"For the failures among these students the blame is not all on one side, but the larger responsibility is ours, and it is high time that the nation and the church realized what the situation is and comprehended the test and opportunity which it presents."

Speer concluded his remarks by saying that "the church may find in these thousands of students missionaries to carry Christianity back to their own people. They will not carry back what they do not get, and they will not get what we cannot or do not give."

If we give them materialism and an "every-man-for-himself" mentality, it would be better if these international students had never come to this country. Even if we give them the best education available and skills to help their people, we're still not making a lasting impact on society.

But if we give them Jesus, we're giving them everything.

They will take something home from America. What they do take is up to you and me.

Chapter Thirteen

Principles to Live By

Over the years, as Rose and I have grown closer together and closer to God, we have discovered that there are certain principles God expects every Christian to understand and follow. We have taught these principles to our children, and Rose included them in her book, *Friends of God*, which was published by Maranatha Publications in 1983.

All of these principles might also be called "laws" in the same way there are laws of nature. For instance, the laws of nature that God put into effect declare that spring follows winter, and that day follows night. We also know that if we want to grow a certain type of food, watermelons, for instance, we have to plant watermelon seeds. In the same way, if we want to have friends, we have to plant the seeds of friendship by seeking to *be* a friend to others.

This, as we will see later, is the Principle of Sowing and Reaping: you will reap what you sow. If you truly seek to serve and esteem others above yourself, you will find that they will seek to serve you and will hold you in high regard. Of course, the opposite is true, too. Anyone who treats others with disrespect and unkindness will find that the Principle of Sowing and Reaping assures he will be paid back in kind.

All of God's principles are positive in nature. If they are understood and applied, they can bring success and joy into your life. They will revitalize your relationships with others, especially with God. But if you ignore them, try to find your way around them, or fight against them, you will only be hurting yourself.

Learning to live by God's principles is a very important step in the life of any Christian, just as it is important to develop faith, compassion, or the ability to hear the voice of God.

These principles are:

1. The Principle of Christian Individuality.
2. The Principle of Self-Government.
3. The Principle of Christian Character.
4. The Principle of Christian Stewardship.
5. The Principle of Sowing and Reaping.

I want to take the time now to discuss each one of these briefly and tell you how they can and should operate in your life.

First, *the Principle of Christian Individuality.* This means that there is nobody else like you. God made you one of a kind and He made you the way you are for very special reasons. No one else can ever take your place. No one else will ever have the special blend of talents, abilities, and experiences that equip you to do the job God has called you to do.

I talked earlier about the young woman I spoke to in the theater who was about to commit suicide. What was her main problem? She thought she was worthless. She didn't understand her importance as a unique human being. She thought she was an insignificant one among billions and that no one would even miss her if she were gone. But that wasn't true.

She was someone created in the image of God, someone for whom Christ died. Once she came to understand that, she had a better appreciation of herself. The Bible says that God is aware when a single sparrow falls to the ground (Matthew 10:29). When you realize that the God of the universe cares that much about a sparrow, you begin to understand just how much He cares about you.

Another thing to keep in mind is that even your negative experiences have helped make you unique and, if you will allow them to, even they can become positive forces for God in your life. When you look back over your life I'm sure you see some unhappy or embarrassing incidents. That's true for all of us. But now these incidents can give you additional insight, compassion, or understanding regarding the problems of others.

For instance, if you were abused as a child, that's a terrible situation, and God never intended for it to happen. But because it did, you can better understand the plight of the abused child, and work to help others who may find themselves in that situation today.

You are a completely unique individual, different from any other man or woman. Have you ever thought about just how unique you are? Whenever I stop to think about it, it makes me feel a special sense of awe for the One who designed us all! For instance, no one else will ever have your exact fingerprints or footprints. No one else will ever have your face or be able to perfectly duplicate your voice. A professional forger might be able to do a good job of copying your handwriting, but an expert could tell the difference.

Human beings are like beautiful snowflakes: No two are alike.

We are all "designer originals." Most of us buy our clothes from the local department store. We go shopping and if we see something we like, we try it on. There may be several suits or dresses just like it. They're mass-produced and that helps to keep the cost down. But how much more would you pay for a dress or a suit personally designed for you by one of the world's great fashion designers? You'd pay ten to twenty times more than you'd pay at the department store. That's because the fashion designer gives careful attention to every detail of his creation. He cuts no corners, and seeks to make everything exactly the way it ought to be. That's the way it is with human beings, too. God is the great designer, and He has built us all with exacting precision and detail.

Now the Principle of Individuality must not be confused with any sort of "individualism." While individuality reflects our uniqueness as human beings, individualism is the idea that "I'm going to be my own person and I don't care how anyone else feels about it." Individualism is a man-centered excuse for selfishness, while individuality exalts God as the designer and creator behind man's uniqueness.

The Principle of Individuality stresses that a person's uniqueness is revealed only as he submits completely to God's will and God's Word. Only by submitting totally to God can you discover the purpose for your unique life.

This principle also stresses the importance of the individual in bringing about change in society. It is the opposite of collectivism, which leads to the philosophies of Communism and socialism.

We talked earlier about the fact that one person can make a difference in society. But, for some reason, most people don't think that way. It's always "we" will make the difference or "we" will reach this world for Christ. We must work together, yes, but our attitude ought to be "I" will make the difference, and "I" will reach this world for Christ. The collectivist mentality stresses the importance of the group effort and considers individual achievement to be of little consequence. The Bible teaches that all Christians together make up Christ's Body, but that every individual has a unique role to play within that Body.

In 1 Corinthians 12:12, Paul writes: "For even as the body is one and yet has many members, and all the members of the body, though they are many, are one body, so also is Christ." Throughout the rest of that chapter the apostle talks about the various members of the Body and the roles they play—each one recognizing its place and function so that the Body works together as a unit.

True individuality will express itself in Christian unity. As the Bible says in Ephesians 4:15–16: "But speaking the truth in love, we are to grow up in all aspects into Him, who is the head, even Christ, from whom the whole body, being fitted and held together by that which every joint supplies, according to the proper working of each individual part, causes the growth of the body for the building up of itself in love."

In summary, then, to recognize the Principle of Individuality is to recognize that you are a unique, special creature, endowed with special gifts and abilities by your Creator. It is also to understand that because of these unique abilities you are called to play a very special role in the Body of Christ—a role that no one else can fill.

Second, *the Principle of Self-Government* has to do with self-control and upright behavior. If you are self-governed you don't need a policeman watching you to make sure you don't break the law. Suppose a high school class is taking a test and the teacher is called out of the room to answer a telephone call. All of the students know that the master test with the answers is in his top drawer. If they are self-governed that knowledge won't make any difference. It is wrong to cheat, and they won't do it.

God wants us all to be governed from within through the indwelling Holy Spirit. At the same time, He allows us to choose whether or not we will accept this internal guidance. If we are not governed from within, by God's Spirit working in our lives, then we will be governed from without, by laws, rules, policemen, armies, and so on.

Proverbs 16:32 puts it like this: "He who is slow to anger is better than the mighty, And he who rules his spirit, than he who captures a city" (NAS). If you rule over your spirit, you are a self-governed individual, and because of this you will be able to accomplish great things for God.

Suppose you are facing an unpleasant task. Do you put it off until the last possible minute? Or do you plunge right in and get it done? Are other people always having to bail you out because you didn't do your part? Or are you the sort of person everyone else can count on? If you are self-governed, you will be a self-starter, a person with initiative and drive.

Have you ever heard someone say, "Well, that's my personality. That's just the way I am"? Some people are almost proud of their laziness. But it's not really a matter of personality: It's a matter of whether or not you are self-governed. You can become self-governed by yielding to the Holy Spirit. Then you will understand what God wants for you, how He wants you to live. And you will seek to live that way, not out of fear, but because you want to please Him.

I was driving down the highway with my family in the car and my foot became a little "heavy" on the gas pedal. I felt a little hand tap me on the shoulder. It was my daughter, Stephanie.

"Daddy," she said, pointing to the speedometer, "you're not being self-governed."

A quick glance at the speedometer revealed that I was going nearly seventy miles an hour.

"Oh, I'm sorry, honey. You're right," and I dropped back down to the legal limit of fifty-five.

If I am self-governed I won't drive seventy just because I don't think there are any highway patrolmen around. I'll drive the legal limit because I know it's the right thing to do.

Now breaking the speed limit may sound like a little thing, but it's only the beginning. Take a look around you, read the headlines in your morning newspaper and you'll see the results of living without self-government: crime, violence, pornography, sexual perversion.

I will never forget what I ran into when I went to start Maranatha fellowships in Australia. At Melbourne University there was such a radical element present that the homosexuals and Marxists had practically taken over the entire campus. They had elected their people to most of the campus offices and the homosexuals were flaunting their deviant behavior in a celebration of "Homosexual Days." They were openly exhibiting the paraphernalia they used in their sexual perversions. The only word I can use to describe it is *gross*. It was hard to believe that anyone could be so debased and so proud of it.

The problem was that these people were not self-governed at all. They did whatever they felt like doing, whenever they felt like doing it, and they didn't care what anyone else thought about it, including God.

Wesley Steelberg had gone with me on that trip, and we began speaking out against that sort of behavior and stressing obedience to God through Christ. Naturally, we had to oppose the homosexual community and call such behavior sinful.

I was preaching to around three hundred Christian students in the student union when the homosexuals and Marxists invaded the place. Some fifty or sixty of them tried to break the door down and began chanting "Fascists go home," so loudly that I couldn't continue my sermon.

What was the reaction of the Christian students? Well, if they hadn't been self-governed their reaction might have been to strike back against the protesters. But, instead, we tried to put our arms around them and tell them we loved them even if we did disagree with the lifestyle they had chosen. I didn't get to finish my sermon that night, but I know that the radicals saw some pretty effective preaching in the actions of these young self-governed Christians.

The Marxists were not through. The next night they were back again and this time things did get violent, but not with us. The university posted several policemen outside the hall during our meeting and when the protesters tried to break the door down, the police moved in. Thankfully, no one was seriously hurt, but the incident illustrated the spiritual truth that those who refuse to be governed internally will have to be ruled through application of external force.

In Sydney we found the same thing. The radicals had the university there in a stranglehold. But in both cities, the believers went to work and through their unified efforts were able to change the universities completely. They actually took over the student government at both campuses, turning out the controlling homosexuals and Marxists. Revival broke out on both campuses.

It's not just non-Christians who fail at self-government: Many Christians live that way, too. And some Christians who *are* self-governed attach to it the wrong attitude: They act out of fear, thinking, "God will get me if I do that so I'd better not do it!" They have never learned to give God His rightful place in their lives, to do what He wants simply because they love Him and want to please Him. Perhaps they have never really submitted their wills to God, and they may even resent Him while they try to serve Him. That won't work.

A self-governing individual has the ability to work diligently without being distracted. He rules over his own spirit and prioritizes his time according to what God wants done. He will not be interrupted by items of less importance until he has finished the task at hand. In contrast, a person who is not self-governing often can't decide what to do first. He spins among projects, never getting very far on any one of them. He has to have someone standing over him telling him what to do, and if his parents, teachers, or bosses leave him alone, he won't do much of anything!

There are three characteristics that are the hallmarks of the self-governing individual: initiative, diligence, and industry.

Initiative means being self-motivated, self-starting.

Diligence is perseverance in any activity.

Industry is a combination of initiative and diligence to the point where they are a natural part of the personality.

If we, as Christians, are to assume the roles God desires for us as leaders and shapers of society, then we must learn to be self-governing through obedience to the Holy Spirit.

Hugo Grotius (1583–1645) wrote a poem that expresses the situation perfectly:

> *He knows not how to rule a Kingdom,*
> *that cannot manage a Province;*
> *Nor can he wield a Province,*
> *that cannot order a City;*
> *Nor he order a City,*
> *that knows not how to regulate a Village;*
> *Nor he a Village,*
> *that cannot guide a Family;*
> *Nor can that man Govern well a Family,*
> *that knows not how to Govern himself;*

Neither can any Govern himself
unless his reason be Lord,
Will and Appetite her Vassals:
Nor can Reason rule unless herself be ruled by God,
and wholly be obedient to Him.

The third principle I want to talk about is *the Principle of Christian Character*. As Christians we should seek to reflect the character of Jesus Christ. To do this we must allow the Holy Spirit to operate in our lives.

Galatians 5:22–23 tells us that the fruit of the Spirit is "love, joy, peace, patience, kindness, goodness, faithfulness, gentleness, self-control; against such things there is no law" (NAS). If you are yielded and obedient to the Holy Spirit, your character will begin to reflect these nine characteristics.

There are many other Bible verses that show us what a Christian's character should be like:

I urge you therefore, brethren, by the mercies of God, to present your bodies a living and holy sacrifice, acceptable to God, which is your spiritual service of worship. And do not be conformed to this world, but be transformed by the renewing of your mind, that you may prove what the will of God is, that which is good and acceptable and perfect.

Romans 12:1–2, NAS

In James 3:17–18 we read that those who possess Christian character should reflect the wisdom of God, wisdom that is "first pure, then peaceable, gentle, reasonable, full of mercy and good fruits, unwavering, and without hypocrisy."

In contrast to this, those who do not possess Christian character will reflect a pseudo-wisdom, which, according to James 3:15, "is earthly, natural, demonic."

The Principle of Christian Character is formed through obedience to God. As we learn—through God's grace and the working of His Spirit within us—to resist behavior that is not in accordance with God's will for us, we will begin to reflect the nature of Christ automatically. Please remember this is nothing we can do on our own, but only through the Spirit of God working within us. The Principle of Christian Character thus goes hand-in-hand with the Principle of Self-Government. As we learn to be self-governing, we will begin to reflect true Christian character.

We also develop Christian character by spending time with God, by learning what He is like, and by doing our best to be like Him. Spending much time in God's Word is also a key. His Word is like a mirror that shows us both who we are and who we ought to be.

Psychologists tell us that it takes about forty-five days to develop a new habit in anyone's life. We all need to develop the habit of spending time in God's Word. Set aside a certain time each day when you'll read the Bible. Don't let anything keep you from it, but note it on your calendar and vow that you'll remember. After those forty-five days, it will become a habit—second nature to you—and you'll wonder how you ever got along before you started spending this time in God's Word. The Bible says in Amos 3:3 that two people cannot walk together unless they agree. In Hebrew *to agree* means "to make an appointment." In order to walk with God, we need to agree with Him—that is, make an appointment with Him—every day.

The Israelites often rebelled against God, and this was due primarily to the fact that they had never come to know Him. They knew His acts because they'd seen the plagues, the parting of the Red Sea, and so on, but they had never come to know Him as a Person. Moses, on the other hand, knew God and talked with Him on a personal basis. When Moses came down from Mt. Sinai after spending time there with God, the people were afraid to look at him because his face reflected the glory of God (Exodus 34:29–35).

Only by spending time with God, and by being obedient to Him, can we begin to reflect His character. There is no shortcut. God does not just zap you and turn you into a holy person. Christian character comes only through obedience to the Holy Spirit and the revealed Word of God.

A person who is strong in Christian character will act

according to what his conscience tells him, and his conscience should always be in tune with the will of God. Because a person of Christian character does what He knows God expects of him, he will be able to stand in the face of danger, hardship, and suffering without compromising.

If you want to see Christian character in action, look at the Soviet Union. Christians there are persecuted from all sides, yet they refuse to denounce their Lord. Look at the poorer areas of the world where Christians are risking their lives to battle poverty and disease. Look at the political arena where Christians are willing to take unpopular stands and risk public humiliation because they will not compromise their faith.

Those who demonstrate Christian character are the true heroes of the faith, wherever they are and whoever they might be. They demonstrate it every day in dozens of ways, both great and small. The man who suddenly realizes the grocery store clerk has given him $10 too much in change and returns it demonstrates Christian character. The young girl who won't listen to gossip about someone else demonstrates Christian character. So does the teenager who refuses to attend a pot party, even though all of his friends make fun of him and call him a nerd.

You can be sure of one thing: those who demonstrate Christian character will always be misunderstood by those who belong to the world. They'll be called "stupid" and "unrealistic" and the world will try to drag them down.

One night back in the '70s while I was still pastoring in Paducah, the Ku Klux Klan held a rally at a five-acre farm on the outskirts of the city.

Bob Nolte, who was still a television reporter at the time, phoned and asked if I would like to go out with him as he filmed a news report from the rally. I felt that it might be possible to do some good, so I went.

Bob and I were both shaken when we got there and saw the potential for violence. The Klansmen had finished with their ritual cross-burning and were now holed up in a farmhouse. There must have been fifteen state police cars on the scene, and all the policemen had their riot guns trained on the

Klansmen. We could see that some of the Klansmen had guns, too. The police had let it be known that if the Klansmen weren't out of that house in a matter of minutes, they were coming in to get them. It was, to say the least, a tense situation.

But what made it worse was that so many of the reporters there were actually trying to incite violence. It was a miracle that the shooting hadn't started already. Some of them were yelling insults at the Klansmen to provoke them into action and others were egging the police on, urging them to "give the guys what they deserve."

Bob spoke to several policemen and asked if we could go in and talk with the Klansmen. They weren't sure at first. Who knew what was going to happen? We might get caught in the middle of a crossfire, or we might wind up being taken hostage. But Bob persisted, and when they realized I was a Christian minister they agreed finally to let us go.

Both of us were praying as we walked across the field to the farmhouse to meet with the men in white sheets, but both of us knew we had no choice if we were going to be the peacemakers God had called us to be.

They met us at the door. "Listen," we told them, "the police are going to come in here, and they are armed to the teeth. But if you'll give up your guns and come out, there won't be any problem."

At least they were listening. There was some loud murmuring, and someone wanted to know if we could guarantee it. We went back and talked to the police.

"There's not going to be any fighting," I told them. "The peace of God will be here and no one will be hurt."

Now some of the reporters weren't too happy about things. A few of them argued that it was a trick, that we couldn't be trusted, and urged the police not to listen to us.

But we finally got both sides to agree. The Klansmen put down their guns, came out of the house, and we led them to the police where they surrendered peacefully.

I asked Bob later if he was frightened during our encounter with the Klan. Now that he thought about it, yes, he supposed he was. But he didn't have much time to be frightened while it was happening. All he knew was that God would have him act to avert violence, so that's what he did.

I know that God was well pleased—and Bob received a commendation from the Kentucky State Police.

That is the Principle of Christian Character, standing up for what you know God wants you to do, no matter how great the odds against you might be.

The fourth principle is *the Principle of Christian Stewardship*. This means that we, as Christians, are called upon to take good care of the things God has entrusted into our keeping. We know that we are to take dominion over the earth, but we must realize, at the same time, that the entire universe belongs to God and not to us. We are to take dominion in His name, and not in our own.

All that we are—mind, soul, and body—belongs to God as does everything we own and everything we do. All must be used to bring glory and honor to Him.

I believe that the human conscience is the most sacred of all the property God has entrusted to man's care. As the conscience is in tune with God's Holy Spirit, it will either accuse us of wrongdoing or let us know that we have done the right thing. The Bible tells us, in 1 Timothy 1:5, that the purpose of instruction is "love from a pure heart and a *good conscience* and a sincere faith."

The Bible also says, "Having a hope in God . . . that there shall certainly be a resurrection of both the righteous and the wicked. In this view, I also do my best to maintain always a blameless conscience both before God and before men" (Acts 24:15–16, NAS).

And again, we find that those who don't know God may "show the work of the Law written in their hearts, their conscience bearing witness, and their thoughts alternately accusing or else defending them" (Romans 2:15).

How can I keep my conscience clear before God? Simply by living as He wants me to live. If I try to maintain a pure conscience, I will know when I have done something wrong and I will immediately confess that sin and seek God's forgiveness. If I continue to ignore my conscience when it tells me I've done something wrong, after a period of time it will become numb. Then it won't hurt me anymore. I can do all sorts of things against God's will and won't even stop to think about them. Anyone can allow his conscience to become calloused and hard. But if you are following the Principle of Christian Stewardship, you will not allow this to happen.

In addition to striving continually to keep our consciences clean, this principle also calls us to speak out against whatever we know to be wrong or evil. If I fail to speak up when people have violated God's Law I am, in essence, agreeing with them.

Could Hitler have massacred millions of innocent people if all the Christians in Germany had spoken out against it? Would the more recent atrocities of Cambodia and Uganda have been allowed if Christians around the world had spoken out? And, bringing the situation closer to home, why don't more believers speak out against the crime of abortion on demand?

I talked about the confrontation with homosexuals in Australia. I had no choice but to point out that their behavior was wrong scripturally and oppose them. Had I failed to do so my conscience would have told me I had done wrong. If you see someone in sin and don't do anything about it, you share the sinner's guilt.

The final principle is one that is stressed time and again throughout the Bible and one I mentioned earlier: *the Principle of Sowing and Reaping*. The truth of this law can be seen everywhere in nature. If you plant corn, you won't harvest tomatoes. If you want to grow a healthy lawn, you won't plant dandelion seeds.

It works that way in the physical world, and it works that way in the spiritual world as well.

As Paul says:

Do not be deceived, God is not mocked; for whatever a man sows, this he will also reap. For the one who sows to his own flesh shall from the flesh reap corruption, but the one who sows to the Spirit shall from the Spirit reap eternal life. And let us not lose heart in doing good, for in due time we shall reap if we do not grow weary. So then, while we have opportunity, let us do good to all men, and especially to those who are of the household of the faith.   Galatians 6:7–10

Most of the time, when people talk about sowing and reaping, they do it in a negative way. If a man has been a troublemaker all his life and now he's in some desperate situation, people say, "Well, you reap what you sow." But it works in a positive way, too. First of all, if you sow good things, if you treat people well and you're kind and generous, then you will reap good things, and people will be kind and generous to you. And secondly, if you go around sowing the seeds of the Gospel, you are going to reap a harvest one day.

If you want your friends and loved ones to come to the Lord, you ought to be planting those seeds in their lives. Remember, seeds don't germinate overnight and it takes some longer to grow than others. But with proper care they will grow.

Remember, too, that the crop that comes in is much bigger than the tiny seeds you planted. Giant oaks grow from tiny acorns. Jesus told the parable of the mustard seed, which is the tiniest of seeds but produces a magnificent tree. In the same way, one kind thought may produce many beneficial actions—and one evil or lustful thought can produce many evil actions.

We must be very, very careful to watch what kind of seeds we are planting. Whether we want to face it or not, harvest time is coming!

So these are five principles in operation in the lives of Christians, and which we would all do well to remember as we walk with the Lord from day to day and as we seek to make a difference in the world for Him.

There is one other important thing to keep in mind as you adhere to these principles. It has to do with the way Christians think. We will make the sort of impact we need to make on society only when we begin to understand that we must reason from the *whole* to the *part,* instead of the other way around.

Most Christians reason from the part to the whole, especially when it comes to winning the world for Christ. What do I mean by this? Simply that they first see themselves as individuals, then they see their part in the local church, their particular denomination, and so on.

God, on the other hand, reasons from the whole to the part. Jesus said in John 3:16 that God "so loved the world" that He gave His only begotten Son. You see, God reasons from the whole world down to the church, down to the individual. I believe we can be deceived by reasoning from the part to the whole. It limits our vision and it keeps us focusing on our own local situations instead of reaching out to all the world.

When we in Maranatha talk with people about Christ, we don't only tell them that Jesus will save them from their sins and that they'll go to heaven when they die. We tell them that they're being saved for one reason, and that is to go into all the world and preach the Gospel, to help reach the 2.5 billion people who have never heard of Jesus.

We must enlarge our vision to include those billions of lost souls.

Consider the Genesis account of creation. The Bible says that God made light and saw that it was good. Then He made the earth and seas, and again He saw that it was good. And as He went on making the various parts of creation, He saw that each part was good.

But, then, verse 31 of the first chapter says: "And God saw all that He had made, and behold, it was *very* good." The parts by themselves were "good," but everything together working in harmony was "very good."

Many churches aren't doing what they could be doing to reach the lost because they are reasoning from the part to the whole. They are shortsighted and selfish. Why are they putting a majority of their budgets into building new sanctuaries and improving programs for their own members when more than fifty percent of the people in this world have never heard of Jesus Christ?

If they would learn to see the whole purpose of God, to work for the entire, eternal purposes of the Father—oh, what a difference it would make!

The typical church person asks, "Where can I go to get my needs met? Where can I go to be blessed? Where can I find the church of my choice?" But that sort of thinking isn't biblical. You know, I used to think "attend the church of your choice" was in the Bible. But it's not. It's in the yellow pages. Instead of asking those questions and focusing on my needs and my wants, I should be asking, "Where can I be of service? Where does God want me to be? What is the most I can do to get the Gospel out to those 2.5 billion who are lost?"

We Christians all need to roll up our sleeves and get busy for His Kingdom. We need to get concerned about His world, and then we can be concerned about our fellowships and our local churches. And the result is that each individual will be blessed.

Until we do, missions work will continue to get the crumbs. Lord, increase our vision!

Epilogue

Maranatha, Today and Tomorrow

We at Maranatha are involved in several exciting projects designed to reach the lost and usher in the Kingdom of God. I want to tell you just a little bit about some of those projects:

The Forerunner

The Forerunner newspaper was established in the spring of 1981, and today it goes out to more than 35,000 students every month. *The Forerunner* is designed to serve as "a prophetic voice to the nation." It's an "issues-oriented" newspaper and tackles and explains some of the toughest issues facing our country today. We talk about what's going on in Central America and especially in Nicaragua; we talk about economic issues, politics, strategies for evangelism. We have correspondents all around the world who keep us abreast as to what's going on in their regions, and we attempt to get at the issues behind the headlines.

The Forerunner is the result of instructions the Lord gave me when I was ministering on the campus of the University of California at Berkeley. Rose and I were walking hand-in-hand across the campus when I felt the Lord telling me, *Just as the* Berkeley Barb *was started to sow seeds of destruction into the youth of America in the '60s and '70s, so I am raising up a* Forerunner *to sow seeds of greatness into the young people of America.*

I wasn't sure at the time how to begin publishing a newspaper, but I knew God wanted it done. In addition to students, *The Forerunner* goes to congressmen and senators, Supreme Court justices, and even the President. We have letters on file from major world leaders telling us that they read *The Forerunner* and benefit from it. Other letters have come from all around the world, thanking us for what we're doing with *The Forerunner* and urging us to continue the good work—and we intend to.

We believe that the written word is extremely powerful and that we can change the conscience of the world through it.

We take our newspapers onto campuses and put them into bins right next to the campus newspaper, and they disappear practically overnight. People are hungry to hear the truth.

People always express surprise when I tell them we have a total of three people on the staff headed by editor Lee Grady.

That we are succeeding in this mission is demonstrated by the letters that pour into our offices every week.

For instance, a man from Guyana wrote us saying: "I cannot afford to miss a single issue of *The Forerunner* because it has inspired and encouraged me as a youth leader in my walk with Christ. Sometimes I feel discouraged and am ready to throw up my hands in despair. But when I read your paper, particularly the testimonies of young people all over the world who are serving God, I feel very uplifted."

A letter from a college student said: "There are a few of us here who are praying for revival to come to our small college of 1,300 students—and we want to see this revival spread to the teachers as well. . . . We need to know what is going on in the Kingdom of God! I want to share your newspaper with other students and faculty here!"

An English teacher from the University of Missouri wrote to

say he wants to use *The Forerunner* in his classroom. So does a professor from a university in Caracas, Venezuela.

From Trinidad, a pastor wrote to say: "I believe your vision to 'take the lead in the battle of ideas' is admirable and truly reflects the concept of the Church being 'the salt of the earth' and 'the light of the world.' You may rest assured of our prayerful support."

And on and on it goes, as letters testify to the impact *The Forerunner* is having all around the world.

The Forerunner Television Show

An outgrowth of *The Forerunner* newspaper has been The Forerunner television show, which was first broadcast over the Trinity Broadcasting Network in 1984.

We've put together a fast-moving, high-tech show that appeals to young families and professionals. The Forerunner TV show packs testimonies, American Christian heritage features, and preaching into a half-hour package. We also feature special filmed reports put together by Bob Nolte that tell of dramatic salvation experiences and chronicle the lives of Christians who are making a difference for Jesus Christ. The show's main purpose is to bring people into a saving relationship with Jesus Christ, and we have many letters testifying to the fact that this is what it's doing.

One young woman wrote to say that she was on the verge of suicide—in fact, she was getting ready to slit her wrists—when our program came on. What she saw on our show not only changed her mind about taking her life, but gave her eternal life in Jesus.

A viewer in Maryland wrote to say that he had been neglecting God for some 25 years . . . "but now I want Him to come into my life. I have been looking for peace of mind and body/soul. I know now that God is the only way."

Another letter, from a young woman who had had an abortion several years previously, wrote to say she had been touched by a program dealing with abortion. She wrote, "The Lord used this program to help me release much hurt. . . . I know my God loves me and . . . I am truly assured again of His hurt for my pain."

In the Philippines, we tried to get The Forerunner on one of the major networks, but they wouldn't let us have any air time. So Rice Broocks, who is my co-host on the program, flew into that country to preach and do outreach, and he talked to the owner of the network. Before Rice was through, that owner and his entire family had met Jesus in a new way! After that, he couldn't wait to have our show on his network, so he pulled another program, and put our show on at an excellent time on Saturdays.

A young woman who is married to an airman stationed at Clark Air Force Base in the Philippines wrote to say that the program "sure helps keep my heart on fire for Christ."

Maranatha Satellite Prayer Network

It was also in 1984 that the Maranatha Satellite Prayer Network went on the air.

Beginning in October of that year, churches from throughout the continental United States began joining together every other month through our Satellite Prayer Network to pray and intercede. Later that year we expanded to include churches in Canada, Mexico, and Hawaii.

We have had as many as two hundred churches joining together at one time to pray for the things that are on the heart of God.

We also joined together to pray against the Mafia. We felt God was telling us that He was grieved by the stranglehold organized crime had on much of this country, and that He wanted us to pray against it. After we did, we started seeing news reports about many arrests being made. During the next twelve to eighteen months after we started praying against the Mafia, there was an awesome succession of arrests.

We've prayed against the drug traffickers and we've seen an increase in the number of arrests made in that area, too.

We prayed for baby Ryan Osterbloom in the hospital and on our Satellite Prayer Network. He was in desperate need of a liver transplant. A donor was found and the successful transplant was performed.

There's an interesting story behind that. I was on my way to the White House to meet with President Reagan when I heard the news about this baby. His mother had even made an appeal to the President, asking him to announce the need for a liver. When I was at the White House I asked one of the President's aides what had happened about this and was told that Mr. Reagan's planned speech had been changed at the last minute, and there would be no mention of the child.

I appealed to them and asked them to please mention the need for a liver for this little boy. I don't know whether my appeal had anything to do with it, but the President did mention Ryan in his speech to the nation that day. Following that, Mrs. Osterbloom appeared on the satellite with us to tell her story. And then the baby received a liver.

We meet together the first Friday of every other month to ask the Lord what He would have us pray about. We will start at 9 P.M. and pray until 1 A.M. And we have seen again and again that the Lord will answer the prayers of His people.

This is a part of what Maranatha is doing, but there's much more.

Providence Foundation

Through the Providence Foundation, we are taking some of the best and brightest students from around the world and training them in the biblical principles behind government and politics. These students are learning the proper role of government as God intended it, and they are learning Christian principles to help them govern wisely. We fully expect that those who have studied in the Providence Foundation will soon be assuming roles of leadership throughout the world.

Our Christian Statesmanship Program is also getting young people involved in the governmental process, including finding jobs for them on Capitol Hill. Politics has sometimes been considered a "dirty" word, but we're excited about the prospect of seeing these godly men and women running for public office. They won't be seeking their own furtherance or promotion, but rather to govern as God would desire.

Champions for Christ

We have started a new organization called Champions for Christ designed to reach out to athletes with the Gospel. We're using films, one-on-one evangelism, and seminars, and many top athletes are giving their lives to Jesus.

A. C. Green, the starting power-forward for one of the best teams in the National Basketball Association, the Los Angeles Lakers, was saved through our ministry at Oregon State University. Today he is part of our church at the University of Southern California and is doing a tremendous job of bringing a living testimony of Jesus to the National Basketball Association.

In an interview with columnist Doug Krikorian, he explained how his belief in God affects his play:

"God wants His people to be warriors—to be battlers and fighters. And I don't mean. . . getting into fights. What I mean is . . . doing as well as you can in your chosen occupation. I don't think any Christian should be a passive kind of person. If he is, then he's going to be headed for a lot of problems in his spiritual walk."

Greg Ball, who is the U.S. director for Champions for Christ, was instrumental in Green's conversion. Green described how Ball introduced himself one day and in "five minutes, he told me pretty much what was going on inside my heart. . . . I had a wrong concept of Christianity. He told me things about myself that day that were incredibly true. It was as though the Lord had told him something about me."

During his career with the Lakers, Green has improved to the point where he is now considered a major reason for that team's phenomenal success. Green's answer to those who have been surprised by his performance?

"The Bible says, 'That which a man sows is what he shall reap.' What that means is that if you're willing to put your time into something, you'll get something out of it."

When A.C.'s playing days are over, he plans to enter the ministry on a full-time basis.

Another member of Champions for Christ is Clarissa Davis, who starred for the University of Texas women's basketball team.

She talked about her relationship with Christ in an article published in *The Forerunner:*

". . . On December 17, 1986, in Miami, Florida, my whole life changed. I had received three consecutive Most Valuable Player honors, and I was averaging 27.4 points and 12 rebounds per game. I felt like I was on top of the world. However, I was not prepared for the rude awakening that was about to interrupt my lifestyle. I went down with what I thought was a simple ankle injury, and the next day I couldn't walk on my foot. What I thought was just a sprain turned out to be much more serious—and I had to sit out for two months and watch everyone else play.

"Needless to say, I was devastated. I felt so empty. I began to close myself off from other people and became rude, arrogant, and selfish. I was sinking deeper and deeper in self-pity, and I kept saying to myself, 'Why me? What did I do to deserve this?'

"Several weeks after my injury, however, I found the answer to my problem. A very special person shared with me about the love of Jesus Christ and how He gave His life for me. I realized that I had offended Christ by putting sports and myself before Him. It made me sick when I saw how selfish I had been. Suddenly I understood that all my materialistic goals could not compare to the most precious thing in life—having a personal relationship with the Lord.

"Jesus changed my life immensely. From that moment my thinking began to change. I no longer looked at sports as being a way to get attention for myself. Now, I used sports to glorify God, realizing that it is only because of Him that I have been blessed with athletic ability. Also, I have stopped putting myself—my thoughts, my emotions, and my will—before Christ. He is number one in my life and I thank Him daily for saving me from a life that was headed for destruction.

"Athletics is going to open doors—but this time those doors are opening so that He can be glorified. He is going to use me to share His love with many others. I want people to know that nothing in this world can satisfy them or fill the emptiness that they feel in their hearts. Only Jesus can do that—and my life is living proof of that fact!"

Creation Science Clubs

We have also established Creation Science Clubs on campuses all across the country in which young Christian scientists are encouraged to continue in research that will support the Bible. These clubs are bringing Christian scientists together where they can fellowship, discover that they are not alone in their beliefs, and that there is a stronger scientific basis for believing in creation than in evolution. We believe these clubs will have a major impact on the scientific community, and show that Christianity and true science are perfectly capable of walking hand-in-hand. The Gospel is a friend, not an enemy, of science, despite the attitude of much of the scientific community.

Maranatha World Leadership Conference

One of the most exciting things we do is host the Maranatha World Leadership Conference in which thousands of Christians from around the world join together to worship and discover new methods of evangelism. We have had the late David du Plessis, Pat Boone, Pat Robertson, Jack Hayford, James Robison, and Kenneth Copeland speak to us—all great men of God.

Maranatha Leadership Institute

And then there is our Maranatha Leadership Institute, where future leaders of our churches undergo intensive training. This is a sort of "finishing school" for our pastors prior to their ordination.

Maranatha Missions

We are also more active than ever before in our missions programs. Every summer we send out anywhere from five to fifteen missions teams, involving hundreds of students and, as we grow, we will increase those numbers. Our goal is to send teams to every country on earth. We also support orphanages in several countries.

Wherever we go, and whatever we do, we always seek to follow God's leading.

For example, I was praying, asking the Lord how to go about reaching students in Latin America. Then one night the Lord woke me up and told me that He wanted me to have a film produced in Latin America, featuring Latin Americans, and showing what God was doing in their lives.

So I wrote the idea down, submitted a budget, and eventually we signed Bob Cording to travel throughout Latin America with evangelist Luis Palau. We asked Palau if he would co-sponsor the project with us, and we ended up with a beautiful film. We've been able to have it broadcast on TV, we've taken it into theaters, and we've even set up a projector in a town square and shown it on the wall of a nearby building! Every time we've shown it, dozens of young people have come forward to give their lives to Jesus.

Maranatha Publications

And then there's Maranatha's publishing arm. So far, we've sold more than 400,000 copies of our books, and it's all grown from a comment one of the members of a Bible study class I was teaching in Paducah made to me.

247

Every Tuesday night I used to teach a two-hour class on the Bible. Each week I would print up a lesson plan and hand it out to my class. One night after the class one of the students came up to me and said, "Bob, you ought to put these lessons into a book."

I had never thought of that but it made a lot of sense, so that's what I did.

We published *Bible Studies for a Firm Foundation* and *Bible Studies for the Overcoming Life*. We also published a series of booklets by Lee Grady, with titles such as "Science and the Bible," "A Vision for World Dominion," "War of the Words," and "Defending Christian Economics" and others.

One of the dearest things to Rose and me is our *Friends of God* children's book. We were discouraged when we began looking around to see what Christian books were available for children, because we just didn't see anything that taught the principles we wanted to teach them. So Rose began putting together a series of Bible stories, and we commissioned an artist to do fifty-seven original oil paintings.

The final product, *Friends of God*, includes Bible stories that are broken down into short segments. Each segment contains several questions designed not only to discuss the content of the Bible stories, but to teach children how to reason from a set of given facts, uncover biblical principles, and relate those principles to everyday life.

MotherLetter

Another important ministry is our MotherLetter, which is edited by Bob Nolte's wife, Diana, and goes out six times a year to Christian women all over the world, helping them build stronger marriages and families. The MotherLetter includes scriptural wisdom and serves as a forum where Christian women can share their special insights and victories with others.

These are some of the various aspects of Maranatha, and I could go on for some time yet. But I'm sure you get the picture by now of what we're all about.

But whatever we do, it's done with one thing in mind: to spread the Gospel of Jesus Christ.

My life is full and busy, but it also involves a tremendous amount of fun and excitement. I've experienced firsthand the joys of being a disciple, and I wouldn't trade it for any other kind of life.

Those of us at Maranatha believe in our name. We believe that Jesus is coming back soon, and that's why we're working so hard to get ready.

Jesus says, "Behold, I am coming quickly, and My reward is with Me, to render to every man according to what he has done."

And again, He says, "Yes, I am coming quickly!"

Amen. Even so, come, Lord Jesus.

For more information on
Maranatha and its ministries,
contact:

Bob Nolte
Director of Ministry Relations
Maranatha Campus Ministries
P.O. Box 1799
Gainesville, FL   32602

or call us at
904-375-6000